RICHARD PEIRCE

PANGOLINS

SCALES OF INJUSTICE

This book is dedicated to all those fighting for a
future for the world's most trafficked mammal.

Published by Struik Nature (an imprint of
Penguin Random House South Africa (Pty) Ltd)
Reg. No. 1953/000441/07
The Estuaries No. 4, Oxbow Crescent,
Century City, 7441 South Africa
PO Box 1144, Cape Town, 8000 South Africa

Visit www.penguinrandomhouse.co.za and
join the Struik Nature Club for updates,
news, events and special offers.

Ebook first published in 2020
Illustrated ebook published in 2021

Printed edition first published in 2021
1 3 5 7 9 10 8 6 4 2

Publisher: Pippa Parker
Managing editor: Roelien Theron
Editor: Helen de Villiers
Designer: Janice Evans
Proofreader: Thea Grobbelaar
Typesetter: Deirdré Geldenhuys

Reproduction by Studio Repro
Printed and bound in Hong Kong

MIX
Paper from
responsible sources
FSC
www.fsc.org
FSC® C144853

ISBN (print): 9781775847120
ISBN (epub): 9781775847137

Cover: The eye looked through me, in me, and around me. (Jen Guyton)
Title page: Enigmatic, enchanting and almost prehistoric. (Wendy Panaino)
Opposite page: Exploring on an accompanied evening walk. (Ashleigh Pienaar)
Contents page: Hungry and out foraging in broad daylight. (Wendy Panaino)

CONTENTS

Will Clothier

AUTHOR'S NOTE

This book is, of necessity, a mixture of fact and fiction. The events described and the stories told are fact based, and where there are gaps I have kept as close as possible to what is likely to have happened. Many of the characters gave permission for their real names to be used, but in other cases, either for legal reasons or because names are not known, I have had to use fictional names.

All of the lead characters have read the manuscript and agreed that events described were as true as they could be, and whenever I have had to use my imagination, I have based my story on true events that unfolded in similar situations.

Ray Jansen along with the other men and women on the armed frontline of the battle to save pangolins are not only brave, they are largely unsung heroes. It's my hope that this book goes some way towards thanking them for what they do and acknowledging their efforts. The quiet, dedicated determination shown day after day, week after week by the pangolin carers, veterinary and otherwise, matches the work of the sting and enforcement teams, and together they represent a chance for these beleaguered animals.

Pangolins have impressive claws for digging.

FOREWORD

BY PROFESSOR RAY JANSEN

Founder and Chairman of the African Pangolin Working Group

Pangolins are the most mystical and bewitching creatures, often mentioned as cultural omens and in tales associated with phenomena of weather, witchcraft or fortunes of luck. Being the only mammals covered in hard, keratinous, overlapping scales, these rare animals have only been sighted in their natural habitat by the very fortunate few – often a fleeting glimpse at dawn or dusk but nevertheless a sighting and an experience of a lifetime. Being shy, predominantly nocturnal, solitary, territorial and quiet, they are one of the very rarest sightings anyone can have. With no teeth but a very long sticky tongue, almost the length of their own body, pangolins seek out their favoured ants and termites – lapping up thousands with every feed. Their eyesight is generally very poor but they compensate with excellent hearing and an exceptional sense of smell, having the ability to scent out favoured food nests well below the surface, excavating termitaria and ant nests with very strong, well-adapted forelimbs.

Only recently have pangolins been the focus of extensive research as we still understand very little about their life history, ecology, reproductive biology, physiology and evolutionary history. However, it is an exciting time as the world is starting to take notice of these rare and elusive mammals and multiple studies are currently under way around the world where scientists are revealing the fascinating ways of pangolins. I have been very fortunate and blessed to be granted the privilege of working with and studying these truly wonderful, peaceful mammals.

Pangolins unfortunately hold the title as being the most sought-after traded mammals in the world. They are a prized dish in countries such as Vietnam and their keratinous scales are ground up into powder and used as an ingredient in a multitude of cultural Asian remedies. Such has been the demand for pangolins and their scales in Asia, that the four Asian pangolin species now face a very real possibility of extinction. Being very hard to source as numbers have been depleted over much of their Asian range, the onslaught on the African species has grown exponentially in recent years. Shipments of pangolin scales from the African continent reflect this onslaught. In 2019, alone, 97 tonnes of loose scales were intercepted leaving the African continent; this equates to more than 160,000 African pangolins destined for traditional cultural practices of the East. If one considers that these intercepted consignments represent a very small proportion of the actual undetected trade, African pangolins face a bleak future.

South Africa is only one of the African countries where we experience this illicit trade in pangolins. In this account, Richard Peirce brings the plight of pangolins into homes around the world through the story of 'Zambezi', one pangolin I retrieved in a covert operation into the wildlife trade. Richard brings to life a very real account of what transpired and the journey of this fortunate young male pangolin. He highlights some of the wonderful people and organisations helping pangolins and those undertaking ground-breaking research into these mystical creatures, such as the work Wendy Panaino and her team are doing in the Kalahari. This narrative takes readers to Vietnam and exposes first-hand the blatant availability of pangolins and pangolin products to willing customers – further highlighting the incredible persecution these peaceful mammals face. A sobering conclusion to the book is the Covid-19 novel viral pandemic that has engulfed the world and brought humanity to its knees. Its ironic origin was likely a mammal, possibly an Asian pangolin, in a wildlife market in Wuhan, central China. Mankind needs to urgently revise the use of the earth's wild animals, plants and ecosystems to the benefit of all organisms that share this fragile and unique planet.

RAY JANSEN

Pangolins are thought to have split from the Carnivora some 87 million years ago.

FOREWORD

BY IZAK KRUIPER

The words in this Foreword are not the exact words of Izak Kruiper. They have been taken from a recorded interview with Izak and read to him for his approval. Izak is a Khomani San Bushman elder who lives near Tweerivieren in the South African Kalahari.

'In my culture the pangolin is a revered and sacred animal. It is an animal of peace and calm that does not hurt other creatures – it eats only ants. We do not kill or hunt pangolin. If we find a dead pangolin we use the scales to treat stomach problems, and for people who have seizures. First, we roast the scales in the fire, then we grind them down and mix the powder with water and plant extracts. Seizures and stomach problems are upsets, and the pangolin is calm, so the influence of the pangolin calms upsets.

'We believe the pangolin is related to the wind. If you follow a pangolin to his burrow then sit and wait for him to come out, the wind will put you to sleep. While you are asleep the pangolin can come out and you will not find it. It is difficult to follow or find pangolins because the wind will wipe out their tracks.

'The pangolin is also closely related to the tortoise. When we sing the pangolin song there will be peace and rain. The wind, which is a friend to us and the pangolin, will bring the rain. When the new moon appears we sing the pangolin song. Three to four days later, when the moon is changing and lying on its side like a bucket that holds the rain, we take a tortoise and we eat the meat, and sprinkle the blood on the fire. The wind will carry the sparks and smoke up to the skies and rain will come. Also, to make medicine, we grind up tortoise shell and mix it with the scales from a pangolin that has died.

'If the pangolin were to disappear it would be very sad because we believe the spirit of the pangolin is everywhere and in us. If someone kills a pangolin, that is very bad, and from then on, that person will always have bad luck. Even if that person is sorry afterwards, the pangolin is still dead, and the curse lasts forever.

'I know that many people now want pangolins. If you find one, they are easy to catch because they roll into a ball and you can pick them up. I have been asked by non-San people to catch pangolins and they will pay me money, but I said "no". You should not kill a spirit for money – money has an end, but the spirit does not. Selling a pangolin for money would mean the pangolin would die, which means you helped kill it, and you will have bad luck forever.

'A while back we were often approached by people who asked us for pangolins but they don't ask any more because they know we will say "no". I know other people are catching pangolins and this is very bad; the pangolin is sacred and walks with the wind.

'I am happy for your book. I hope it does good for the pangolin – they are a calm and peaceful creature, hurting no-one.'

IZAK KRUIPER

IZAK KRUIPER

Dylan Smith

ACKNOWLEDGEMENTS

Academic Press – *Pangolins, Science, Society & Conservation*

Alexis Kriel

Angie Dube

Anton Leach

Arnold Meyer

Ashleigh Pienaar

Clawed Hat Films

Charlotte Peirce-Gregory

Denise Headon

Don Pinnock

Duncan MacFadyen

Dylan Smith

Eye of the Pangolin (film)

Gordon Greaves

Izak Kruiper

Jacqueline Peirce

Jagged Peak Films Ltd

Jasmine Duthie

Karin Lourens (Dr)

Karl Ammann

Kjell Bismeyer

Lisa Fanton – author of *Pangolins*

Lisa Hywood

Malveen Manyeta

Matthew Adams

Mika – the cat

Michelle Panter

Neil Britton

Nguyen Van Thai

Nicci Wright

Rachel Love Nuwer – author of *Poached*

Ray Jansen (Prof.)

Simon Naylor

Steve Leonard

Stewart Muir

Suzi Manley

Tswalu Kalahari Reserve

Valery Phakoago

Wendy Panaino

Wilfred Chivell

And, finally, thanks to everybody at Struik Nature who once again dealt with a difficult author with patience, and did a brilliant job putting this book together – Pippa Parker, Helen de Villiers, Janice Evans and Belinda van der Merwe. I apologise to anyone I have inadvertently left out.

ACRONYMS

CITES	Convention on International Trade in Endangered Species of Wild Fauna and Flora
COP	Conference of the Parties (to CITES)
DRC	Democratic Republic of the Congo
KZN	KwaZulu-Natal
IUCN	International Union for the Conservation of Nature
MERS	Middle East Respiratory Syndrome
NPC	China's 'National People's Congress'
RBD	Receptor Binding Domain
SARS	Severe Acute Respiratory Syndrome
SFGA	China's 'State Forestry and Grassland Administration'
TCM	Traditional Chinese Medicine
TOPS	Threatened or Protected Species
WHO	World Health Organisation
WPL	China's 'Wildlife Protection Law'

A pangolin emerges from its burrow.

PREFACE

Lisa Hywood is founder of the Tikki Hywood Animal Trust, a 24-hour rescue and rehabilitation facility in Zimbabwe that cares for smaller and lesser-known animals. She describes her first encounter with a pangolin: 'I opened this sack and inside, this one eye – and I remember it distinctly as if it was happening right now – this one eye looked at me, and it just looked through me, in me, and around me. This one eye, and time froze for me and I was in that moment humiliated, ashamed, and saddened that I was a human being. It was horrendous and it was as if a knife just went through my heart; how could we as an intelligent species allow this to happen?

'I have had a lot to do with many animals, especially elephants, but this was an animal that spoke more volumes in silence, with one look, than any other animal I have ever had an interaction with. That look changed everything, and that rescued female pangolin was the beginning of my life with pangolins.'

Lisa has a no-nonsense air about her and has clearly seen the good, bad and ugly of wild animal conservation in Africa. The above quote was delivered with commitment and passion; and in the same way that Lisa had been influenced by the eye of the pangolin, when I interviewed her, her gaze drew me into her world – the world of the most trafficked mammal on the planet. A pangolin's whole body is covered in scales, and the eye of the rescued animal that looked at, into, through and around Lisa was both accusing and questioning. And the question was 'Why?'

Over 97 tonnes of illegally shipped scales from African pangolins were intercepted being exported into Asia in 2019. An estimated 1,900 pangolins are killed for every one tonne of scales, and extrapolating from those figures, a staggering 160,000 pangolins were illegally shipped from Africa to the Far East in 2019. These figures are based, of course, only on what was intercepted, and so represent only a part of the total number of pangolins killed for the Asian market.

Pangolin scales are made of keratin, which is a protein, and the scales are similar in composition to rhino horn – or human fingernails, or hair. A kilogram of pangolin scales is valued at $3,000: the armour that nature gave these animals for their protection has now become the very reason for their having become one of the most trafficked wild animals on earth.

I did many interviews before I met my first pangolin. When I asked people to tell me about these animals and why they are special, all their answers contained similar and unusual descriptive threads. The eyes were always mentioned, and the animals were themselves described as being magical, bewitching and like no other creature.

I met my first pangolin in Johannesburg Wildlife Veterinary Hospital. He was lifted out of his day cage and carried to scales to be weighed. He was only slightly curled up and his head was fully visible. I wanted eye contact, I wanted to feel the magic and get drawn into the mystique. The daily weighing preceded the evening feeding walk, and this pangolin was quite relaxed and almost looked as if he was enjoying being handled. Maybe he just knew the routine, and knew that he would soon be out of his cage and feeding. Whenever possible while this was going on I made eye contact; I looked at him and he looked at me, and I understood. The eye of the pangolin transmitted many messages: vulnerability, innocence, yet at the same time almost wisdom, and trust and calm were also there. These animals have a significant place in many African cultures, and in some are regarded as being sacred, magical, mystical and bewitching. I am not sure these are the right words, but I spent two hours that evening accompanying the pangolin on his feeding walk, and by the end of my time with him I was hooked. Pangolins are very, very special, and by the time we parted company I was doubly convinced that we must fight and exert every effort to stop them being trafficked to extinction.

RICHARD PEIRCE
October 2020

PANGOLIN FACTS

- Pangolins have been on earth for about 80 million years, and moved into Africa approximately 40 million years ago.
- There are eight different species of pangolin in the world: four are found in Africa and four in Asia.
- The four African species are the Black-bellied pangolin, White-bellied pangolin, Giant ground pangolin, and Temminck's ground pangolin. The four Asian species are the Indian pangolin, Philippine pangolin, Sunda/Malayan pangolin and the Chinese pangolin.
- Pangolins have important cultural significance in many African communities.
- Pangolins are not related to sloths, anteaters or armadillos, to which they may bear some superficial resemblance.
- The word 'pangolin' comes from the Malay word *pengguling*, which means 'roller'. This refers to the animal's natural defence posture of rolling itself into a ball when attacked or startled by potential predators or other threats.
- Rolling themselves into a tight ball not only effectively wraps their scales around their soft, vulnerable underside, but the scales themselves are sharp and can easily cut attacking or investigating predators. Pangolins can also emit a pungent putrid fluid from their anal glands to repel attackers.
- Pangolins are the only mammal with scales; depending on the species, these comprise about 20% of their total body weight.
- The gestation period lasts 70–150 days, and varies between species.

- Pangolins usually give birth to only one pup for each pregnancy. At birth, the pup's scales are soft, but they soon harden.
- None of the eight pangolin species has teeth. They use their very long sticky tongue to eat termites and ants. When feeding, they can constrict their nostrils to keep ants out.
- A pangolin tongue can reach up to 42 centimetres (±17 inches) when fully extended.
- Pangolins have an excellent sense of smell but very poor vision and hearing.
- They are largely nocturnal and mostly solitary.
- Temminck's pangolins are bipedal, walking mostly on their hind legs, while using their forelegs and tail for counterbalance.
- Pangolin scales are made of a protein called keratin, as are rhino horn and human nails.
- There's an insatiable demand in China and the Far East for pangolin scales for use in traditional medicine, making the scales, at $3,000 per kilogram, one of the most sought-after items in the illegal wildlife trafficking sector. The pangolin is now the most trafficked wild mammal on the planet.
- In addition to the demand for their scales, their meat is also considered to be a delicacy in China and Vietnam, which further increases the pressure on these species. Pangolin meat sells in Vietnam for $300 per kilogram.
- In China, pangolin scales are prescribed for the treatment of cancer.
- Pangolin wine is produced by boiling rice wine with a baby pangolin. The wine is purported to have various healing properties.

An adult Philippine pangolin and her pup in the forests of Palawan, Philippines

PART 1
ZAMBEZI

Above: Every rescue and return to the wild has a
special place in Ray Jansen's memory. (Ray Jansen)
Previous spread: The capsule with a blue flashing light helps
minders keep track of the animals when they are out feeding.

CHAPTER 1

AN UNLIKELY HERO

A bearded professor of ornithology from the Tshwane University of Technology might seem an unlikely candidate for a gun-toting hero on the front line of a wildlife war. But Professor Ray Jansen, chairman of the African Pangolin Working Group, is just such a hero. He has become a specialist in 'sting' operations, which he sets up to rescue live pangolins from poachers and traffickers – a racket that has seen pangolins become the most trafficked mammals on earth.

Ray Jansen works in collaboration with units from a special section of the South African Police Service called the Stock Theft and Endangered Species Unit. These highly trained armed intervention units provide Ray's police backup and the arrest capability that he hopes will end with poachers heading for conviction and jail.

At first glance, this tall, slim, almost gangling academic doesn't seem to fit the hero bill. However, closer examination reveals determined dark eyes and an unwavering, steady gaze. His walk is purposeful, his movements economical. He served in the South African Defence Force, and later on in a Special Forces unit; the skills and determination he learned in this training now have a new focus – rescuing poached pangolins and returning them to the wild. Ray is determined to help save these targeted African mammals, one animal at a time. He is not such an unlikely hero, after all.

Ray has been studying African pangolins for more than a decade, investigating and publishing his findings on the bushmeat trade and cultural use of pangolins in West Africa, the ecology of Temminck's ground pangolins in southern Africa, pangolin parasitology, the evolutionary genetics of African pangolins, and the rehabilitation and release procedures necessary for pangolins retrieved from the illegal trade. His primary role as a scientist and academic pays his salary, but his involvement as an agent fighting the wildlife trade of pangolins drives his passion.

It was Wednesday, 9th October 2019, and Ray was near the climax of his latest sting operation – one that had already involved a couple of false starts, making all the players even more jumpy. Alone, he sat in his Haval vehicle in the parking lot of the Kolonnade Mall on Zambezi Drive in Pretoria, his senses heightened and his nerves on edge. Waiting for the contact, his thoughts ranged over the sequence of events involved in setting up this, his current rescue operation. He again ran through his planning and preparations, searching for any flaws or mistakes that might jeopardise a successful outcome. On the seat beside him lay his 9mm Beretta semi-automatic pistol, which had a 15-round magazine capacity. To a degree, the presence of the weapon was a comfort and provided reassurance. But he had been in action before and was all too aware that no matter how well armed or trained he was, it would take just one bullet from someone else's gun – and, for him, it could all be over.

Andries Burger, also alone, was sitting in his Toyota Hilux. He had been contacted four days earlier by a man offering to sell him a pangolin. He had no idea why he had been selected for this contact. He guessed it might have been because he had a large new vehicle, ran a lodge on a reserve in northern Limpopo, was known to have a love of wildlife and, to an outsider, probably looked rich. He supposed that someone had put all these facts together and decided he was worth approaching to buy a rare animal. His guess was wrong – he had been approached by mistake! The wildlife trader who had contacted Andries, initially by 'Messenger' on Facebook, had, quite simply, been given the wrong person to contact. In fact, the reserve on which his lodge was situated had been identified as a good potential place for poaching activities, and the intention had been to point out Andries as someone to keep an eye on, not someone to get in touch with.

Andries had contacted his local police when he first received the offer to buy the pangolin. Early on, it had become apparent that the trafficker wanted to do the deal in the Pretoria-Johannesburg area, so Andries's local police contact had passed him on to the police in that area. They, in turn, had contacted Ray, the pangolin sting expert, and given him Andries's details. Ray and officers in the special Stock Theft and Endangered Species Unit had briefed Andries thoroughly on the various steps that would be involved in the sting. Ray himself was usually the buyer, but today Andries had that role and, when summoned by Andries, Ray would play the part of his money man.

Andries now sat parked in the same car park, but on the opposite side to where Ray was waiting. Like Ray, Andries was under no illusion that things could not go wrong, and if they did, he knew he could find himself in a very dangerous situation. He knew from Ray that three of his previous 22 stings had involved shots being fired, and he hoped this operation would not be number four. He had once been in the South African Police Service himself and knew that, in stake-out situations, the waiting was the worst part.

Ray's wife often asked him why he did this, why he was prepared to risk his life and his family's future. Now, as he sat and waited and pondered these issues, the answer was abundantly clear: he was hooked, as hooked as any heroin junkie. Pangolins had invaded his being and stolen his heart and soul, and rescuing them was now his prime aim in life.

He sat alone with his thoughts, checked his watch, touched his pistol, and waited. He now needed to clear his head and sharpen his focus; to be in the right frame of mind to produce the ruthless efficiency of action that would ensure that he and Andries achieved a successful rescue, and survived whatever might happen.

Ray and his police colleagues were not the only ones waiting that lunchtime. At the Johannesburg Veterinary Wildlife Hospital, pangolin rehabilitation specialist Nicci Wright and her veterinary colleague Dr Karin Lourens knew that Ray was running a sting, and that, if it went well, they would soon receive a new patient.

The Limpopo River defines the border between Zimbabwe and South Africa, and it was across this river that the pangolin was smuggled.

Across the Limpopo River, hundreds of kilometres to the north of where Ray sat in his vehicle, a young Matabele family awaited the return of a loved one – their husband and father. This family man was on a trip into South Africa, and they hoped he would return with money to feed and clothe them and buy the expensive medicine needed for a sick child.

The final piece of the jigsaw was the pangolin, which lay curled up in fear and discomfort, wrapped in a large piece of old cloth. The unfortunate animal was jammed together with other items in the boot of a vehicle that was making its way towards the rendezvous point where seller would meet buyer. The South African middleman was driving, beside him sat an associate, and behind them sat the poacher from Zimbabwe's Matabeleland – the family man so anxiously awaited back home. And behind them all lay the curled-up pangolin, which would soon be the centre of attention and even be given a name.

A rescuer eases a trapped, tightly curled-up pangolin out of a plastic bag.

The natural habitat of the pangolin is increasingly given over to farming, such as in this rural scene in Zimbabwe. The encroachment of humans exposes the animals to the constant threat of capture and trafficking. (Dooshima Tsee)

CHAPTER 2

MATABELELAND

Joseph Themba Khumalo lived with his family in a small village called Juta, close to Lutumba, a much larger, and rapidly expanding village in Zimbabwe's southern Matabeleland. When he was 18, he had married his 15-year-old girlfriend from the village. Their first child, a girl, had died soon after birth; two sons and another daughter had followed, but one of his sons had a weak constitution and was often sick. They regularly had to take him to the government clinic at Nuli, and sometimes even the private clinic at Lutumba, and were often told the boy needed antibiotics. Government supplies of drugs were in short supply, and although antibiotics were available at the private clinic, they were expensive and beyond the reach of the family.

Like many others in his area, Joseph eked out a subsistence living from the land and a few animals: chickens, sheep, goats, two cows and patches of maize kept his family alive. It was a life of grinding poverty. Drought, disease and other dangers were always lurking in the background, threatening their continued existence.

Joseph's wife, Siphiwe, had been a pretty, precocious 15-year old. Now, four children later and 23 years of age, she looked much older. Gone were her slim body and ever-present cheeky grin, and in their place was a more solid woman, now with serious responsibilities that sometimes gave her a world-weary appearance.

Siphiwe was deeply religious. She prayed regularly for a little help from God for all her family, and particularly for her sickly young son. She was a good mother and wife. Her domain was her yard and the four huts that bordered it. The young family lived with Joseph's mother, father and grandmother. Age usually rules, but Siphiwe was a tough, strong-willed young woman and she, not her parents-in-law, was the dominant force in their world. She did her best to ensure that the round kitchen hut and three square living and sleeping huts were kept as clean and tidy as possible.

Her family's diet consisted of pap and green vegetables twice a day, and, with no gas or electricity, meals were prepared on open fires. The whole family helped with the daily chores of collecting water, as well as harvesting wood for cooking and heating.

Siphiwe had become friendly with Angie Dube who was a nurse at the government clinic in Nuli. Angie, who was only five years older, had completed her education and studied hard to qualify as a nurse, and now worked for the government health service. She had become Siphiwe's health mentor and her influence was present in every facet of the way Siphiwe cared for her children and ran her household. The younger woman clung to Angie's every word, and the nurse's positive influences had considerably improved the young family's quality of life and chances of survival. Siphiwe didn't want or expect much, and followed the nurse's advice, while praying for a small miracle that would help her family and make their lives safer and easier.

Beitbridge, on the border with South Africa, was only a few kilometres to the south, and many of Joseph's and Siphiwe's friends and members of their families had crossed the border in search of better lives. Joseph was an intelligent man who knew that nothing was free, and nothing came for nothing. He knew the fallacy of the saying that the streets of South Africa's towns and cities were paved with gold, and it was clear that the country to the south did not necessarily offer easy opportunities. However, the wellbeing of his family and the need for drugs for his sick son both weighed heavily on his mind, whether he was out herding his livestock or at home, lying awake at night in his sleeping hut.

Sitting in the shade of a Musasa tree, Joseph watched his animals making the most of the sparse grazing. He sensed, before he heard, the breathless approach of his five-year-old, eldest son. Their home was just less than a kilometre away, and the boy had run to tell his father to come home at once as a visitor had arrived.

Leaving the child to watch the animals, Joseph told his son he would not be long, and set out at a brisk pace. An old white Toyota Cressida with a South African number plate was parked outside his home, and next to it stood a man he had never seen before. His daughter and younger son were pretending to play nearby, but actually were keeping a close eye on the stranger.

David Masondo had been a wildlife trader and middleman for nearly six years. He had been introduced to the idea of wildlife trading a few years back, when he was taking a group of Chinese tourists on an arranged tour of Johannesburg's Mai Mai area, a traditional South African artisan and medicine market. A Chinese guide in charge of the group had approached David and asked for his help in procuring wildlife items for some of the members of the tour group. Rhino horn, ivory, a leopard skin and other items were on the list, and David had managed to source them all. In so doing, he realised there were healthy profit margins to be made, and this ultimately led to his full-time involvement in the illegal wildlife trade. He now had extensive South African, Chinese and Vietnamese contacts, all of whom were involved in the trade and were part of, or linked to, organised criminal wildlife trading and smuggling networks.

His main contact and best customer was a Vietnamese man for whom David now worked almost exclusively. Pangolins had recently become a priority requirement, and David needed to set about developing his own sources of the world's most traded wild mammal.

During an overheard conversation involving one of his competitors, David learnt that this rival had established a regular source of pangolins from peasant farmers and shepherds in Zimbabwe, and the pangolins were either delivered, or the trafficker went north into Zimbabwe to collect them. It would have been easier, and much less risky, for David to have bought the pangolins from his competitor. However, there were clearly large profits to be made, and David had no intention of taking only a small cut. He had his own buyers and he guarded them jealously; he would not want to pay any middleman. It was this policy that led to his trip to Matabeleland.

He crossed into Zimbabwe at Beitbridge and started making discreet enquiries among local rural populations. Cryptic phone calls, muffled conversations and consultations in the noisy anonymity of local bars had resulted in several leads. Following one of these led David to the village of Jute, and to Joseph Khumalo.

Joseph raised a hand, called a greeting and approached the stranger standing outside his house. David had an open face, a face that said 'You can trust me'. This, his huge grin and outstretched hand combined to make Joseph less wary of the stranger than he might otherwise have been. Introductions followed and David let his silver tongue loose, charming and beguiling Joseph and gaining his trust.

David said that he had heard that Joseph was a good man and was honest and trustworthy, that he worked hard but was poor and could use help from a trusted friend. After a while, David asked Joseph if he would like a beer, and went to fetch a pack of Castle Lager cans from his car. Some hours and many beers later, David finally got to the point: the buying and selling of wild and domestic animals. David produced a photograph of a pangolin, and asked Joseph if he knew where such animals could be found. Joseph said that he knew of two or three likely places, all less than a day's walk from his house. He explained that these animals spend the day underground and that he would have to dig for them. He further mentioned that a friend and neighbour had some hunting dogs, which would be useful.

David repeated an earlier warning that catching, moving and selling these animals was illegal, and advised that Joseph should tell as few people as possible that he was going to catch and sell pangolins. Joseph gave the assurance that he understood the need for secrecy, but that he absolutely trusted his friend with the dogs and wanted him to be involved. David could hardly believe his luck: Joseph was only the third person he had approached, and he seemed to have struck gold. He offered R15,000 (South African rands) per pangolin, delivered anywhere on or near the N1 (the national road to the north) over the border in South Africa.

David produced a large, shiny, state-of-the-art Huawei cell phone. Joseph took out his much smaller, out-of-date Nokia and entered David's number, while silently promising himself that soon he, too, would have a late-model phone. Joseph agreed to call David as soon as he had caught a pangolin. The new partners declared their trust in each other and parted like lifelong friends. Joseph hurried off to find his son, and met him bringing the stock in for the night.

Poverty is a powerful persuader that leaves people like Joseph little choice if they are to survive. Joseph had needed no great persuasion to break the law. His sick son and hungry dependants meant that, when offered a means to make money, he would welcome it and seize it with both hands.

That night, Siphiwe questioned Joseph about what the man from South Africa had wanted. Joseph not only loved his wife, he trusted her absolutely and so he told her everything he had discussed with the South African: the money that had been offered, what he had to do for it, and what the money would mean for their family. Siphiwe listened in silence and when he had finished, she told her husband he would have to be careful, but that this was a chance they should take. Later that night, as Joseph slept beside her, she stared into the dark and wondered if God had sent her a miracle. Then she prayed, thanking Him for this opportunity, and asking Him to keep her husband safe in what she knew was a venture full of risk.

Neither Joseph nor Siphiwe would have thought of it this way, but the scales of injustice were weighted as heavily against them and their family as they were against the pangolins Joseph would soon try to catch and sell.

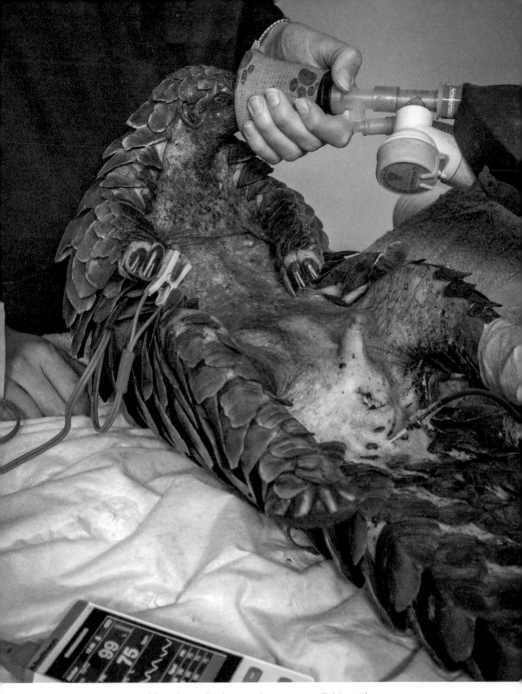

Hi-tech medical procedures are available at the
Wildlife Veterinary Hospital in Johannesburg. (Nicci Wright)

CHAPTER 3
FOR THE LOVE OF ANIMALS

Together with Professor Ray Jansen, Nicci Wright was a founder and director of the African Pangolin Working Group, which was launched in 2011. She is an independent wildlife rehabilitation specialist with decades of experience, during which she has dealt with more than 340 indigenous species. For 16 years she was the Senior Animal Manager at the FreeMe Wildlife Rehabilitation Centre.

In recent years, the rehabilitation and release of poached pangolins has increasingly become her focus. Together with veterinarian Dr Karin Lourens, she is a partner in the Johannesburg Wildlife Veterinary Hospital. Nicci and Karin share an abiding love of, and respect for animals, and particularly wildlife in need of help.

Their hospital treats many wild species, always with the intention that not only will animals be restored to good health, but that they will eventually be released back into the wild. With skills that complement each other, Nicci and Karin's partnership is well placed to tackle the challenges of treating, rehabilitating and releasing the poached pangolins that Ray Jansen and others intercept in their sting operations.

Nicci and Dr Karin

They started their pangolin work at the hospital in 2017. In 2018 they dealt with 43 cases, then in 2019 the number increased to 50. At the beginning, the survival rate was 50%, but by the end of 2019, lessons learnt had pushed the figure up to 85%. They acknowledge they will never succeed with all cases – some pangolins arrive at the hospital too ill to have much chance of survival. The damage can be either physical or mental, or more likely both, and as soon as an animal arrives the veterinary evaluation begins. Within a short time, Karin and Nicci are able to assess which animals are likely to respond to treatment and go on to the rehabilitation process – and which are not. Nevertheless, irrespective of each animal's prognosis, all pangolins are fought for, and many have surprised Nicci and Karin with their resilience and recuperative powers.

The rescued pangolins are trafficked from many regions. Karin and Nicci agree that Temminck's pangolins coming from different areas can have distinctly different characteristics even though they are all members of the same species. They point out that pangolins originating in the bushveld can be different in a number of ways from those that started life in the Kalahari Desert. The Kalahari Temminck's pangolins are smaller than their bushveld brothers and sisters, their scales can be slightly different in colour, and their diets may differ too, reflecting the availability of the ant and termite species in their home ranges. When assessing areas in which to release rescued pangolins, identifying the type of area from which they originate can be vital in ensuring the animal's survival.

Nicci saw her first close-up pangolin in 2007, and, just as with Lisa Hywood, Ray Jansen and others, her first meeting with this mystical, almost mythical species changed her life forever. Karin's reaction was little different – the innocence of the animal struck a chord deep inside her.

Ray Jansen always kept Nicci and Dr Karin informed of his upcoming sting operations. On Monday evening, 7th October, he had called Nicci and told her he was in the middle of a sting and hoped for a result the next day. But that event had failed to take place, and now it was Tuesday

Pangolins use their extraordinarily long tongue
to extract termites from their nests.

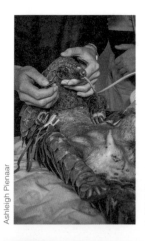

Ashleigh Pienaar

Ashleigh Pienaar

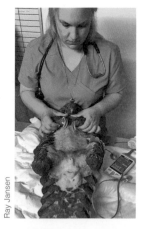

Ray Jansen

Ashleigh Pienaar

Pangolins rescued from traffickers arrive in varying states of health. Veterinary tests and assessments guide treatments, ranging from the painstaking checking of new arrivals, administering treatment where needed and drilling holes in scales to attach monitoring tags. The hospital is always busy. In 2018 they dealt with 48 pangolins, and in 2019 the number increased to 50. As lessons have been learnt, the survival rate has steadily increased.

In the final phase of rehabilitation, pangolins are released every evening
for a feeding walk, each animal accompanied by a dedicated carer.

Ashleigh Pienaar

Young pangolins stay with their mother for up to two years.

evening. The third attempt at catching the traffickers was to take place in the car park of the Kolonnade Shopping Mall on Zambezi Drive in Pretoria. Any top-class professional sportsman will confirm that, on big match days, the waiting is the worst part. Once the whistle goes and the game begins, you are in action and the dynamics of the game take over. So it is with Ray, Nicci, Dr Karin and all the others regularly involved in sting operations. Their individual fears and concerns may vary, but their levels of anxiety are similar.

Ray considered his own and Andries's safety, the requirements of evidence gathering, the safety of his backup team, the state of health of the pangolin and a host of other risks and variables. In the final run-up to a sting, Nicci usually found herself wondering how traumatised her new charge was likely to be; and Dr Karin's mind was full of concerns about medical details such as liver and kidney function, degree of dehydration and emaciation, and blood panels.

These were the thoughts churning in their minds as they all sought to sleep on Tuesday night, each in their own way praying for a satisfactory outcome the next day.

On the night of Sunday, 6th October, Joseph carried an old sports bag containing the pangolin across the border into South Africa. The pangolin was exhausted, traumatised, and curled into a tight ball. He did not understand what was happening to him. All his senses transmitted unfamiliar signals to his brain, so he stayed tightly curled up in his natural defence posture.

Joseph had rung David on Friday to say he had successfully collected the required animal, and would make a plan to get it into South Africa.

As often happens, success breeds greed, and David was no exception. His friends and associates all knew that he made his living in the illegal wildlife trade, and one of his friends had recently given him details for a man who might be interested in buying a pangolin. David had wondered for some time whether his Vietnamese buyer was giving him enough money, and decided to contact this potential new buyer. David didn't know that his friend had misidentified the new contact, and consequently David ended up contacting the wrong man. He had got in touch with Andries Burger.

On Sunday afternoon, while Joseph crossed the border with the pangolin in his sports bag, and Ray and Andries geared up in anticipation of the impending sting, David drove north up the N1. He would stay with a friend in Polokwane, where he would wait for Joseph's call. He was eager to take possession of his first poached pangolin.

David looked forward to the big money he would soon be making, but in spite of these pleasant feelings of anticipation, an irritating little question lurked in the back of his mind and wouldn't go away: everything was going well, but was it going *too* well? Had it all been too easy?

A Temminck's pangolin emerges from its burrow
for a daytime feeding expedition. (Francois Meyer)

CHAPTER 4

TEMMINCK'S PANGOLIN

While the poachers and traffickers planned their next moves, life continued in the bush as it always had. Under a full moon the landscape had an eerie, other-worldly, silvery appearance, an almost lunar feel. The bushes and trees cast sharp shadows, while the brightness of the moon appeared almost to extinguish the myriad stars normally visible from deep in the African bushveld. The night sounds added to the magic of the scene as the creatures of the bush went about their night's business.

When night had well and truly fallen and the moon was at its zenith, the pangolin set off from his shallow burrow on his nightly feeding expedition. The little animal's habitual bearing was low to the ground and so he cast almost no shadow as he explored the terrain in search of ants and termites. In contrast, a stately termite mound in the distance cast a gothic castle-like shadow across the dappled landscape, seeming to serve as a beacon for termite predators. However, no amount of light or its shadows would be of advantage to the pangolin, as these creatures have very poor eyesight. Their hearing is also poor, but they possess an extraordinary sense of smell and it was this that guided the pangolin on his food patrol.

On locating the termite mound, he used his powerful front claws to dig into it, and then probed the insect tunnels with his tongue. His preferred diet comprised a variety of ant species, but tonight he was hungry, and on this particular feeding foray his initial selection was termites, for the food bulk they represented. His saliva-covered tongue probed deep into the tunnels, and every time he withdrew it, it emerged coated with termites trapped on its sticky surface. While eating, he closed his eyes and tightly constricted his ears and nostrils to keep out the multiple insects that swarmed all over his head. In just a few minutes he had reduced one side of the gothic castle to sandy rubble, and he moved on in search of other prey. Pangolins don't have teeth so he

Pangolins are essentially night-time feeders, although hunger drives some to continue foraging during daylight hours. In some places, human encroachment and climate change have degraded their natural habitat, leading to an uncertain food supply.

couldn't chew his food as such, but sand trapped on his tongue helped his powerful mouth in the mastication process. Sand and small stones in his stomach further helped grind his food.

He crisscrossed the savanna surprisingly fast, having switched his search from termites to the more usual ants. He stopped frequently to coat his long sticky tongue with another swathe of prey, and safely deposit the haul in his mouth.

Pangolins had peacefully occupied this land for tens of millions of years. This Temminck's ground pangolin was about nine years old, and had lived his entire, relatively untroubled life in these familiar surrounds in southern Zimbabwe. For now, the moonlight and the wind were his friends, and as the sun rose in the east, he made his way back to the burrow where he would spend the day sleeping and recharging for the next night's foraging expedition. As he went about his nightly feed, nothing about the peaceful landscape, the soft hues of dawn or the constant chirring of cicadas hinted that this had been his last night in the wild for the foreseeable future – that within a few days he would have been captured and transported across a national border in an old sports bag, subjected to life-threatening stress and trauma, and that his very existence would lie in the balance. He would find himself in the trafficking pipeline that pandered to the appetites of wealthy consumers on a far-off continent.

Within a matter of months of his capture, the biggest news in the world would be a virus that started infecting and killing humans in China. Soon, the word 'pangolin' would be on the lips of people worldwide – people who didn't even know what a pangolin was, or what it looked like. Everyone had suddenly developed an interest in pangolins!

Several hundred kilometres to the south, outside Pretoria in South Africa, the traffic fought its noisy way past the Kolonnade Shopping Mall on Zambezi Drive – an address that would soon lend its name to the pangolin from Zimbabwe.

Although sometimes spotted during the day, pangolins
usually emerge to forage under cover of night.

A policeman carefully opens a black bag, exposing two illegally caught pangolins. (South African Police Service)

CHAPTER 5
CAPTURE, TIP-OFF, STING

THIS CHAPTER IS BASED ON ACTUAL EVENTS, BUT FOR LEGAL
REASONS AND TO PROTECT INDIVIDUALS, IN SOME CASES
PLACE NAMES AND PEOPLE'S NAMES HAVE BEEN CHANGED.

THE CAPTURE

Ever since his meeting with David, Joseph had thought of pangolins and little else. His family usually had enough to eat, and they all had some clothes, but there were no luxuries and there was no safety net in case sickness or any other mischance should befall them. Joseph did not like the idea of breaking the law, and he did not like inflicting suffering on animals. If he had to kill an animal, such as one of their chickens, he always did it quickly and efficiently. He liked wildlife and enjoyed wild places; many times when tending his sheep and goats, he would watch wild birds and animals, and he felt close to them.

He had seen pangolins on a few occasions, either very early or very late in the day. He knew they mainly came out at night, and on one occasion soon after dawn he had watched one emerge from a burrow.

The day after his meeting with David he started looking for pangolin burrows and tracks, and identified six burrows that he thought might be home to such an animal. Joseph had considered sitting through the night and watching them one by one, stake-out fashion, until he found his pangolin. But at the thought of the long, lonely nights, he quickly dismissed this idea and instead decided to work with his friend, owner of three dogs.

The plan was to visit all the burrows he knew and see which ones got the attention of the dogs. If the dogs' behaviour suggested a burrow contained an animal, they would dig for it. There was only a tiny crescent moon on Monday, 30th September when they made their first foray. Joseph had picked a night with no moonlight because he didn't like the thought of being conspicuous under a full moon. The chances of their being seen out in the bush in the middle of the night were negligible; nevertheless, Joseph knew he was poaching and was comforted by the cloak of darkness.

On their first night they checked three burrows. The dogs showed no interest in the first two, but at the third, which was quite a large burrow, they started barking, and one of them disappeared down the hole. After a few minutes of digging and scratching noises and underground yapping and barking, the dog came out backwards with a bloody face and porcupine quills in its ear and mouth.

The hunters were out again two nights later on Wednesday, 2nd October, and checked two burrows Joseph had earmarked during his daytime explorations, neither of which got the dogs excited. Setting off on the third night, they were starting to realise that poaching was no easy money-tree. The first hole drew another blank but at the second, the dogs went wild, and had to be dragged back and tied up to stop them digging. Watched by his friend who held the torch, Joseph took the spade and began to dig.

The pangolin had heard the commotion caused by the dogs at the entrance to his burrow. He had gone as far back into the burrow as he could, then curled up and waited. In front and above him he heard thudding and scraping noises, which were rapidly coming nearer. Then the tunnel in front of him collapsed, and he rolled into an even tighter ball as a strange light probed the darkness, and found him.

The burrow had not been deep, and Joseph had not had to dig for long. As the spade broke through into the tunnel, the two men exchanged grins.

Now on hands and knees, Joseph cleared debris and felt his way deeper into the hole. As soon as he touched the quarry, he knew he had struck it lucky. He shifted his weight sideways, half turned around, and handed the pangolin up to his waiting accomplice.

Still tightly rolled up, the terrified creature was placed into an old sports bag with a broken zip, and the men and dogs carried their prize back to Joseph's house. Joseph had modified a small chicken run to hold his captured pangolins. He had scoured their settlement area for posts, wire, and other materials to make the run escape-proof. In the early hours of the morning on Friday, 4th October, still in the bag, the pangolin was lowered into his temporary prison.

Joseph joined his wife in their bed. He told her he had found a pangolin and that it was safe outside, at the back of their house. Siphiwe was glad and thanked God for what she was sure was a miracle.

Both Joseph and his wife knew that what they were doing was wrong. It is easy for lawmakers to be sure about right and wrong, and for righteous armchair critics in rich western countries to be judgmental about poaching. And it is easy for criminals to exploit people made so desperate by poverty that they will knowingly break the law. At Joseph's end of the food chain, life is all about survival, while for David and those further up the criminal network it is all about profit. Lying not 20 metres apart on that night, the pangolin and his captor were both victims of circumstance. Joseph hardly slept; he lay awake, willing the hours to pass so that he could call David and tell him he had a pangolin. He finally made the call at 8.00 a.m. and David answered immediately. He wanted to know how large the pangolin was and Joseph gave a rough estimate. They arranged to meet at Musina – the northernmost town in South Africa – on Monday afternoon, and Joseph was to call on Sunday night or Monday morning to confirm that he had crossed the border.

Joseph's intention was simply to walk across the Limpopo River, which formed the border between Zimbabwe and South Africa. There were many crossing points used by smugglers and illegal immigrants, and Joseph had done his research and chosen the one he would use. It would be a long walk, but he hoped to get lifts along the way. He was aware, too, of the need not to be seen. He decided to set out very early on Sunday morning and cross the border under cover of darkness that night. As far as he knew, the water would be shallow at his chosen crossing point.

The captive pangolin spent most of Friday and Saturday curled up in the sports bag in the modified chicken run. There was water in the run but nothing to eat. During the hours of darkness on Friday and Saturday nights, when all was quiet and he thought it was safe, he explored his prison. He found a few ants but nowhere near what he needed, and as time went on he became very hungry. He tried scratching around in the chicken run, and found some mealie meal crumbs, which he ate, along with sand and grit. When he heard Joseph moving about in the early hours of Sunday he climbed back into the sports bag and curled up.

THE TIP-OFF

The man who had suggested Andries as a pangolin buyer was not very bright. Thabo had operated on the fringes of South Africa's wildlife poaching and smuggling world for several years. Also known as Rasta, he sported dreadlocks and fake Polaroid sunglasses, and invariably wore a Bob Marley T-shirt and faded blue denim jeans.

Thabo already had three criminal convictions, and associating with him was risky, but David nevertheless often used him for low-level odd jobs. When Thabo suggested Andries to David as a possible buyer, he was making a big mistake – one that would have a serious impact on both men's lives.

On Saturday, 5th October, Andries sat at the desk in his lodge savouring his first cup of coffee of the day. He was flicking through messages on his cell phone when he came across a weird one: 'Call me for a special deal if you like pangolins.' – followed by a cell number. A scam, a hoax, or a mistake? He didn't recognise the number and normally he would simply have deleted the message, but on this occasion, for no particular reason, except maybe curiosity, he called the number.

David had half expected that his message would not result in a call, and was surprised to hear an obviously white Afrikaans voice on his phone, asking him what he wanted. He asked Andries if he liked pangolins. Andries was aware that pangolins were being heavily trafficked, and the ex-policeman in him immediately saw an opportunity to catch criminals. When he answered 'yes', the voice at the other end asked if he would like to buy one. He feigned interest and played for time, telling David that he would call him back. As soon as he closed the call with David he phoned the local South African Police Service Stock Theft and Endangered Species Unit to tip them off.

The police encouraged Andries to go back to the contact and move things along: they were keen to set a trap and catch the pangolin poachers red-handed. In a follow-up call it became apparent to Andries that David expected the deal to take place in the Pretoria area – not up north where Andries lived, as had been assumed. David would not say where he was – he would only discuss where they would meet to exchange the animal for money.

When Andries asked about the price of the pangolin, David was initially cagey, merely promising that if Andries liked pangolins, he could get him many more. Eventually David named his price – a whopping R100,000. Andries made a point of laughing out loud on the phone at this ridiculously high price. But they agreed to keep talking, and Andries promised to call back in a couple of hours.

Meanwhile, Andries phoned his police contact and told him the deal would take place not in Limpopo but in the Pretoria area. This was clearly a different police jurisdiction and the Limpopo police put Andries in touch with Ray Jansen and the Pretoria branch of the Stock Theft and Endangered Species Unit of the police. They started putting together a sting operation.

Back in Zimbabwe, Joseph left home at 3.00 a.m. on Sunday morning. He was driven for the first part of the journey by his friend, the dog owner. He had never before been so nervous or frightened; his friend's car was very old and anything but reliable. If the car broke down or they were stopped, he would be caught in possession of a poached animal. Joseph's imagination was in overdrive. On the floor behind his seat were two bags. One contained a change of clothes, some food and water, and a large knife; and the other held a still tightly curled-up pangolin.

Joseph's friend drove him as close as he could to the border, then Joseph got out of the car, slung one bag over each shoulder and set off for the river crossing. He had transferred the large knife from the bag to his belt. He didn't really know why: if he met a crocodile the knife wouldn't be of much use, and if he were stopped by the police, he wouldn't be able to fight their guns with his knife. The weapon was useless in practical terms, but just having it was reassuring and some comfort.

He managed to cross the river, wading waist-deep in places, and then walked for hours, and by the time he reached Musina, he was bone-weary. He called David, who said he would leave immediately to come and collect him. David also checked with him that the pangolin was still okay.

Thabo was with David when he picked up Joseph and his precious cargo, and both South Africans were eager to see what was in the sports bag. The pangolin had by now not fed for three days, had been bouncing around for hours in the sports bag slung over Joseph's shoulder, and was disoriented and exhausted. After being peered at and poked, he was wrapped in a large piece of cloth, and hidden in David's car boot among a clutter of various items.

Joseph was surprised that he was now being 'collected' along with the pangolin. He had expected to hand the animal to David in Musina, get paid and return home. However, David explained that Joseph's share of

Joseph's captive pangolin was one of many being continually trafficked by criminals.

the money would be forthcoming only when David himself had actually been paid; what's more, he needed the extra pair of eyes that Joseph brought to the party. Joseph had no choice but to tag along.

The two South Africans and the herder from Zimbabwe set off southwards down the N1 towards Pretoria and the pay-off they believed was waiting for them.

During Sunday evening and Monday morning there had been lots of calls between Andries and Ray, and between Andries and David. Ray had suggested that Andries agree to a provisional price of R80,000 for a healthy live animal, and a meeting place outside Pretoria had been proposed by David.

They needed a way for Ray to get involved in the deal, and to get his hands on the pangolin, so it was agreed that Andries would meet the seller, inspect the animal, and then call Ray who would pose as the money man handling the cash. As soon as Ray was happy there was a live pangolin, he would signal to the waiting police who would swoop and make the arrests.

Unbeknown to each other, both parties to the deal were heading south down the N1 on Monday afternoon. In the back of the Toyota, an exhausted Joseph slept all the way, while in the front seats David and Thabo discussed their plan for the exchange. Their idea was that David would meet the buyer alone, and Thabo and Joseph would act as lookouts.

THE STING

Monday and Tuesday were days of frustration for Ray, Andries and the police units waiting on standby. In a succession of calls between David and Andries, meeting places were agreed and then changed, and David tried asking for a higher price. This attempt was firmly rebuffed by Andries, who threatened to pull out of the deal. Nerves and tempers frayed, and at times it looked as if the deal would not happen at all.

David and Thabo were old hands at law breaking and were not particularly nervous. Any anxiety they felt centred on being sure they were getting the best price possible for the pangolin, and making arrangements for the handover that posed the least risk of arrest. In their business, the risk of getting caught was ever present, so arrangements had to allow for an escape route, and they needed a place where lookouts could monitor developments and spot a trap or an ambush.

For Andries and Ray, the nervousness was of a different kind. They knew there was a pangolin out there somewhere, and they worried that if the deal did not happen the animal would not be rescued and might die. They also worried that the opportunity to arrest the traffickers would be lost. They did not know who they were dealing with, and the risk of a shoot-out was always in the back of their minds. In his conversations with David, Andries realised he was dealing with an experienced crook, although in some ways he was not entirely professional, a factor that Andries hoped would give law enforcement the upper hand.

On Monday night Andries firmed up plans with David: it was agreed that the transaction would take place on Tuesday morning, 8th October, at 10.00 a.m. The place that David proposed was the KFC outlet in Bronkhorstspruit, which is a small village outside Johannesburg.

David, Thabo and Joseph got there early to work out how to play it. David would meet Andries in the restaurant, Thabo would roam the car park and the general area to make sure that Andries was not accompanied by the police, and Joseph would stay out of sight in David's car with the pangolin. When David was happy that Andries had the money, and Thabo gave the all-clear, David would take Andries to the car, show him the pangolin, receive the money, hand over the animal and everyone would leave. That was the seller's plan.

Andries drove into the KFC parking lot at 10.05 a.m. and went into the restaurant. In and around the car park Ray, along with police from the Stock Theft and Endangered Species Unit, the Bronkhorstspruit police canine unit, and a special Gauteng police deep cover unit were all positioned strategically in unmarked vehicles. They quickly spotted the Bob Marley Rasta patrolling the car park, and making regular cell phone calls as he reported to someone, whom they correctly assumed was David.

The police had been briefed about Ray and Andries's strategy, which was that Andries would meet David, confirm the price and ask to see the pangolin. Then, when he was sure there was a live animal, he would tell David he needed to call his friend to bring the money. Throughout negotiations, Andries had stressed that he would not actually have the money on him, but that once he had seen the pangolin, he would call his friend who would bring the money. This plan was to forestall the possibility that the gang could hold Andries up at gunpoint, take the money and run.

For a successful prosecution, the gang had to be caught in possession of a live pangolin and be in the process of trying to sell it. The possibility of Andries wearing a 'wire' was discounted as being too dangerous. So it was agreed that, as soon as Andries called Ray, and Ray had sight of the pangolin, he would raise his arms in the air, and stretch: this would be the signal for all the police units to close in as fast as possible.

David had told Andries he would be wearing a blue shirt. When Andries entered the restaurant there were three men in blue shirts sitting in different places around the room. However, one of them was with a family and another looked too old; by a process of elimination, the blue-shirted man seated next to an exit door was the likely candidate.

Andries joined him, and they started talking, trying to get the measure of one another. David once again tried to increase the price, a move that was rejected; Andries demanded to see the pangolin and David assured him it was close by. Meanwhile, Ray, the police units and Joseph all waited in their cars, while Thabo continued patrolling and watching. Sometimes he stood in doorways, sometimes he walked around rather obviously looking at vehicles, and sometimes he stood in the open, trying to look as if he were waiting for a friend to arrive.

Just over half an hour after David and Andries had met up in the restaurant, Thabo panicked. Two police vehicles that had nothing to do with the sting pulled into the car park: the weary police officers wanted some KFC and a Coke. Thabo phoned David, told him it was a set-up and that he should run. Thabo closed the call and, as nonchalantly as possible, left the area on foot. Joseph also noticed the arrival of the police, but he read the situation correctly, realised they had come for a snack, and stayed put in David's old Toyota.

David saw Thabo leave, but watched the police and came to the same conclusion as Joseph, silently cursing his over-nervous lookout man. Nevertheless, he made excuses to Andries and, like Thabo, also left on foot. As soon as David had walked out, Ray, the police units, and Andries, one at a time, all left the area without acknowledging each other. David and Thabo were in cell contact, and an hour later they returned to fetch the car and a very worried Joseph.

About an hour later, David called Andries to apologise and ask for another meeting. Andries played hard to get, saying he was not prepared to waste any more time. David seemed desperate as he assured Andries he had the pangolin with him and was keen to close the deal. This time, Andries proposed the meeting place, and suggested the Shell Ultra-City in Midrand, just off the N1 highway at 3.00 p.m. that afternoon.

For the second time that day, Andries, Ray and the police units got themselves into position and waited. Andries was inside the café reading a newspaper over a cappuccino, while Ray and the officers were all in their vehicles. By 3.30 p.m. there was no sign of David or Thabo, and Andries decided to leave. He signalled for his bill and while he waited for it to arrive his phone rang. It was David saying that he was stuck in traffic about 10 kilometres away on the highway, and hadn't moved for over half an hour. Andries said he would call him back. He consulted a traffic app on his phone, which confirmed that David was not only telling the truth, but that he would be delayed for a long while yet. He called David

Crest of the African
Pangolin Working Group

Ray Jansen

An officer decides to investigate a plastic container.

Ray Jansen

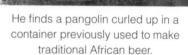

Ray Jansen

He finds a pangolin curled up in a
container previously used to make
traditional African beer.

Ray Jansen

The poachers are made to lie
face-down as the police take
control of the situation.

Ray Jansen

The sting is wrapped up and all
those involved go to the police station
to complete formalities.

back and agreed they would meet in the morning. Even if Andries had agreed to wait that afternoon, David would not have gone ahead with the plan – there was no way he and Thabo would have agreed to meet for the transaction anywhere unless they could get there well in advance to check the place out.

David dropped Thabo off and took Joseph and the pangolin with him to his apartment in the city. Joseph tried to get the dehydrated animal to drink; he knew that a dead pangolin was not part of the deal, and left a bowl of water for the terrified creature when it was shut in the kitchen for the night.

Lying on a mattress on the other side of the kitchen door, Joseph heard scratching sounds in the night as the pangolin used his last energy exploring, in a vain bid to escape. He found the water bowl and had a drink, but there was nothing to eat and no way out.

By morning, the pangolin was once again curled up in the sports bag.

Joseph was woken at 7.00 a.m. on Wednesday by David, who announced they had to leave immediately for the new rendezvous: they were to meet at 9.00 a.m. at the Virgin Active health club at the Kolonnade Shopping Mall off Zambezi Drive in Pretoria North.

Ray, Andries and the police units met at a nearby petrol station at 8.15 a.m. to fine-tune their strategy, and by 8.45 a.m. the police units and Ray had moved into position at the Kolonnade and were waiting. Andries was fervently hoping it would be a case of 'third time lucky', because there had been two false starts and a day wasted, and he needed to get back to his lodge. If this one did not work, he planned to tell Ray he would have to leave.

Meanwhile, David, Thabo and Joseph had arrived earlier for a good look around, and an exhausted and by now very weak pangolin lay in the boot of the car, having once again been wrapped up in the piece of cloth.

Because David and Andries now knew what the other looked like, David had suggested they meet in the car park and not in a restaurant. Andries told him he would be driving a sand-coloured Toyota Hilux, and David said he would find him. David's plan was slightly different in that this time he had decided that both Thabo and Joseph would patrol as lookouts, and call him if they saw anything suspicious.

At 9.06 a.m. Andries pulled into the parking lot, and by chance parked only three cars along from David's vehicle. David watched him arrive but didn't approach immediately – he was waiting to see if Andries's arrival triggered any other activity. He couldn't see anything worrying, and called Thabo and Joseph, who both reported that the coast seemed to be clear.

This time everything went according to plan for the sting operators. David and Andries met up, and Andries asked to see the pangolin. Initially, Andries thought the animal was dead, so David poked and prodded him to make him move. Andries called Ray, who arrived carrying a small 'money' bag, and was also shown the pangolin. He then stepped back, raised his arms in the air and, very obviously, stretched.

Within seconds they were surrounded by police with weapons drawn. Thabo and Joseph saw what happened and ran for it. Warning shots were fired into the air as the police shouted at them to stop and lie down. While the police mopped up the situation, Ray gently picked up the pangolin, took him to his car and placed him in the waiting transport crate.

The arrested men, the police, Ray and Andries then went to the police station to complete formalities. Greed had long since made criminals of David and Thabo, now circumstance had done the same for Joseph; all three men had ended up being arrested, thanks to a mixed message and the market demands in a far-off land. Joseph had gambled by breaking the law in an effort to help his poverty-stricken family – and had lost both his freedom and his family, who would now have to manage without him. All three arrested men faced long jail sentences, and the pangolin faced a desperate fight for his life.

Ray Jansen

Ray Jansen

Ray Jansen

Ray Jansen

Sting operations require careful planning and close coordination among all those involved. Such encounters can be dangerous, with desperate poachers often prepared to defend their trade with the use of weapons. Two defenceless pangolins – the hapless commodity – lie curled up in plastic bags.

And so begins the long road of recovery and return to the wild. (Ashleigh Pienaar)

CHAPTER 6

REHABILITATION, REST AND RECOVERY

The pangolin was frightened and confused. In the last week his world had been turned upside down. He had spent a lot of time curled up in a new world of strange smells, sounds and sensations. He had been losing weight and getting weaker daily. Most recently he had spent over two hours in the boot of David's car, before Ray transferred the terrified animal to the purpose-built transport crate. Now lying on a bed of thick blankets, he was no less frightened, but he was more comfortable and cushioned, and less thrown about in the moving vehicle.

Shortly after 1.00 p.m., Ray and his police escort from the Green Scorpions pulled into the Johannesburg Wildlife Veterinary Hospital (JWVH) where Nicci and Dr Karin were waiting. Accompanied by a police officer, Ray carried the transport crate into the hospital's main treatment room, and put it down on the floor. There then followed a legal process during which custody of the animal was transferred from the Green Scorpions to Ray, and from Ray to the hospital. The officer said his goodbyes and left. Ray, Nicci and Dr Karin had a coffee while Ray explained the details of the sting. Nicci and Dr Karin were eager to open the crate and examine their latest charge, but waiting an extra few minutes gave the pangolin more time to settle, and it was important that they learn all Ray knew about the creature. They would need a name for their newest patient, and all agreed that 'Zambezi' – the street address of his rescue – would be fitting. That it also alluded to the large river defining the northern boundary of the land of his birth made it even more appropriate.

Veterinary staff were now able to unroll him and check the condition of his body.

The pangolin became aware that something had changed. He was not sure what, but all his instincts were telling him that his situation was now different. Perhaps his senses were detecting a new ethos, now of concern, care and gentleness. He knew he had stopped being tumbled back and forth, and was comfortable on the blanket, but he was overwhelmed by feelings of extreme exhaustion.

Ray and the women crossed the room to Ray's transport crate. Dr Karin bent down, unlatched and opened the door, and Nicci reached in and gently picked up Zambezi. They had dealt with 43 rescued pangolins in 2018 and already it looked as if 2019 would be even busier. Handling so many animals had fine-tuned their instincts, and even before conducting an initial visual examination, those instincts told them that this was a very sick animal. The two women – animal care specialist and veterinarian – would now set their familiar assessment routine in motion; and as they did so, the pangolin's chances of surviving the ordeal that had begun six days ago, in another country, took a tentative step forward.

For the time being, Ray's job was done. He said his goodbyes to the two women, confident that he was leaving the pangolin in the best possible hands, and went out to his vehicle. As he drove away, a slight smile tugged at the corners of his mouth. Lou Reed was playing on his car radio, telling him to take a 'Walk on the wild side'. I will, thought Ray, and so will pangolins as long as I have anything to do with it. For him, there are few better feelings than having successfully delivered another rescued pangolin into the hands of those who could offer it a chance of returning to freedom in the wild.

As soon as Ray had gone, the process of health evaluation began in earnest. The pangolin was placed on the floor to see if he could walk properly and was checked for a limp or any obvious injuries. There were various pointers to look out for: for example, a pangolin dragging its tail is a sign of a compromised animal, and a bright and lively animal is clearly in better shape than a listless one. After this brief initial visual assessment, which had not been encouraging, Zambezi was taken to the scales to be weighed, and was then anaesthetised for a series of tests and a thorough veterinary examination. Dr Karin and Nicci were now able to unroll him and to check the condition of his body. His pelvic region showed prominent pelvic bones, his stomach was sunken, and the scales along his sides were caved in instead of sticking out. There was little body fat, he looked gaunt and emaciated, and was almost certainly severely dehydrated. While anaesthetised, he was put on a fluid drip to counter the dehydration. Nicci and Dr Karin estimated that he was probably about nine years old, and they believed that an animal his size, at that age, should weigh about 11 kilograms. At 9.8 kilograms, he was at least a kilogram short of that.

Dr Karin took blood samples and did a full blood panels, in which his liver and kidney readings both indicated a degree of organ failure. Before going home for the night, Dr Karin inserted a tube into his stomach, and through it fed some electrolytes and other nutrients to get his digestive system working again. Once they had done all they could, they put the little creature back into his crate for the night, locked up and walked to their vehicles.

Before saying goodnight, they exchanged impressions and agreed they were more than a little worried about their latest patient. On top of the bad test results, the pangolin was stressed and traumatised. They shared the hope that they would find him still alive in the morning.

Nicci and Dr Karin both arrived promptly at the hospital on Thursday morning, anxious to discover whether their patient had survived the night. They were elated to find Zambezi not only alive, but that his condition had improved: the previous day's medical attention, followed by 14 hours of peaceful sleep, had greatly helped his cause, and when his crate was opened he raised his head and looked up at his audience. Nicci and Dr Karin are fairly hard-bitten animal healthcare professionals, and would not consider themselves as particularly emotional types, but the pangolin's beady gaze brought tears to their eyes.

The next step in his veterinary evaluation was an X-ray. This delivered mostly good news: there was no sign of pneumonia, and he had no fractures. The X-ray did, however, reveal excess grit and sand (as well as mealie meal, which should not have been there) in his stomach. It was not uncommon to find unusual materials in the stomach of rescued animals.

Later that day the blood tests were repeated, and he was given another tubed feed, this time including semi-solid food. Then, to ensure deep rest, the pangolin was sedated again before being returned to his crate.

On Friday, the pangolin was looking still brighter, and the tests were repeated, with steadily improving results. Nicci and Dr Karin began to feel more optimistic, and on the fourth day, decided that their patient should be taken out that evening to see how he would cope with feeding naturally. Pangolins obviously don't understand human speak and can't do backflips, cartwheels or jumping in the air for joy. However, if this pangolin could have understood their decision, he might well have decided to have a go!

Late that afternoon, Nicci took Zambezi from his crate, weighed him, and then fitted him with two little lights attached to the scales on each side of his body. He was being prepared to be taken on a walk in the bush by Nicci so that he could forage and feed naturally, and the two lights would enable her to keep him in her sights.

Nicci set off with the transport crate to a stretch of pristine bushveld, which they used every night to walk their feeding pangolins. The walks are conducted on a one-to-one basis: each pangolin is accompanied by its own personal walker. On arrival, she opened the crate door and lifted Zambezi out. Then she activated the little lights and carried him across the track before gently putting him on the ground.

For the pangolin this was sensational – his superb sense of smell was going crazy. No more antiseptic hospital smells, no more of the pungent and strange petrol fumes that had nearly overcome him in the boot of David's car, indeed no more strangeness. Suddenly his nose and brain were full of natural scents that he had not smelled since his capture by Joseph over a week ago. He zigzagged happily off, and in no time was taking in loaded tonguefuls of cocktail ants. For an hour the pangolin feasted, making up for lost time. And were pangolin faces capable of looking grumpy, his would have done so when Nicci retrieved him from his foraging, carried him back to her vehicle, and placed him in his crate.

That was the first of his regular nightly feeding outings, the length of time gradually being extended on subsequent days until he was feeding for four to five hours a night. All medical tests, now performed with decreasing frequency, showed that his condition was improving. During the next three-and-a-half weeks, he became a firm favourite with everyone at the hospital and they got to know him as an individual character. He knew exactly when it was time to be taken out, weighed and released for his feeding walk. Prior to being taken out of his crate, he could be heard moving around as if impatiently saying 'Come on, hurry up!'. By the end of October he weighed just over 11 kilograms – a good weight for his size and estimated age.

The stress and trauma had been left behind, and now he was a fit, strong, healthy and happy pangolin. But he was not free, and the next step was to plan for his release back to the wild.

Nicci Wright

Nicci Wright

A handler accompanies each individual pangolin on its nightly feeding walk.

Those who work with pangolins often mention their engaging gaze: the eye that looks at you and through you.

Ashleigh Pienaar

Simon Naylor, Conservation Manager on the Phinda Reserve, releases a
rehabilitated and tagged pangolin back into the wild. (Simon Naylor)

CHAPTER 7

FREEDOM IN A NEW HOME

Thursday, 31st October was exactly four weeks since Zambezi's rollercoaster ride had started in Matabeleland. It was also the date that his release papers came through. Ray and Nicci had been discussing the possible release of Zambezi, together with three other rescued pangolins, on the Phinda Private Game Reserve in South Africa's KwaZulu-Natal (KZN) province. In the Zulu language, the word *phinda* means 'the return', and this was appropriate because pangolins had been locally extinct in that area for nearly 90 years. The team had, in fact, already released three other pangolins in the reserve – a signal event marking the reintroduction of the species to Zululand – and were encouraged by the fact that this pioneering group had done well. The introduction of another batch of pangolins would bolster their numbers.

Simon Naylor is the Conservation Manager on the Phinda Reserve, where he has lived with his family for many years. He, Nicci and Ray (whom Nicci had kept briefed on Zambezi's progress throughout the pangolin's stay at the veterinary hospital), bearing in mind the habitats from which the four pangolins had likely been removed, resolved to release them at Phinda.

Once the decision had been taken, it was time to tackle the paperwork and permissions involved. To move animals across provincial borders, permits are needed; in this case, an export permit from Gauteng province, and an import permit to KZN. Nicci has a permanent export permit from Gauteng for indigenous wildlife, which covers Threatened or Protected Species (TOPS), and this includes pangolins. Now Simon set about applying for a KZN import permit. This was received at the end of the month and plans were made for Nicci to drive to Phinda on Wednesday, 6th November, with the four animals.

The six-hour drive to Phinda would stress the pangolins, and to keep the journey as short as possible, Nicci decided to set off only after the heaviest of the Johannesburg morning traffic had died down. By 8.45 a.m. the pangolins were all in their separate travelling crates, loaded into the back of Nicci's Toyota.

Simon's daughter Tamsin had hardly slept on Tuesday night. As soon as she got home from school that Wednesday, she went to find her father to check that the pangolins would still be arriving that day. She already knew that one of the animals was called Zambezi, and decided that he would be her favourite.

Nicci pulled into the Phinda gate just after 4.00 p.m. and headed straight for the camp where the pangolins would be contained during their release programme.

Tamsin was part of the team that had assembled to receive the pangolins. There was a lot to do. The animals would be stressed and hungry after their long car journey, and each pangolin would need to be fitted with two tags: one was a 'very high frequency' (VHF) tag, which enabled location and tracking using telemetry, and the other was a satellite tag, which continuously recorded data received via a satellite link. Pangolins are highly sentient and sensitive animals, and it was essential for their wellbeing that the reception activity on Wednesday evening be conducted with calm, relaxed efficiency.

The satellite tags were set to transmit the general location of the pangolins every hour; the VHF telemetry would provide precise position fixes. The tags were fitted by drilling a small hole in the dorsal scale, and then attaching a tag using a nut and bolt. Each satellite tag weighed approximately 60 grams, and the VHF tags about 30 grams, meaning their combined weight amounted to 1.5% of the pangolin's whole body weight – a sufficiently insignificant load that would not inconvenience the animal.

Zambezi's travelling crate

Technology makes it possible to keep track of the pangolins after their release.

Claws on the forelimbs help demolish anthills and termite mounds.

Releasing the animals didn't just involve opening the doors of the crates and waving goodbye – a system known as a 'hard' release. The pangolins would, instead, have a 'soft' release, which involved a phased operation. The 'soft' release process was now followed for all four animals.

A release site had been selected for each pangolin, and for the first four days of their new life on Phinda they were taken to their individual release sites and allowed to forage-feed for four- or five-hour periods. Tamsin had effectively adopted Zambezi, having elected to be his personal walker, and accompanied him and her father on each of his nightly excursions.

All four animals were weighed before and after their feeding sessions. Weight monitoring and visual observation enabled the staff to check that the animals were adapting to their new home, and maintaining weight and condition. This careful monitoring showed that, initially, none of the released animals was feeding well, and so for the first two or three days they were fed using stomach tubes to supplement their natural intake. However, Simon and Nicci now decided that the continued handling during the 'soft' release process might be stressing the animals and negatively affecting their settling in. After four days of 'soft' release routine, it was therefore decided to give them a last good tube feed and then let them go.

During the soft-release phase, Zambezi had always set off in a westerly direction, which would eventually take him to a rocky, hilly area. What the release team couldn't know was that Zambezi was heading for familiar terrain, similar to that in which he had lived prior to his capture. Now that the decision had been made to move on from the soft-release stage, Simon and Tamsin took him out for his hard release. They found a burrow, put him in it, then moved off a distance and sat and waited. About two hours later Zambezi emerged, and – true to instinct – headed west. Simon and Tamsin silently said goodbye and good luck.

Zambezi fed as he walked. He did not know what guided him but he kept moving west. Even though the rocky terrain that became his new

An extraordinary sense of smell enables pangolins to find
and identify a range of ant and termite prey species

Simon Naylor

Pangolins use a variety of burrows, including natural cavities between rocks.

Ashleigh Pienaar

Forage feeding involves continual exploration.

home range did not have many burrows in it, Zambezi managed to find refuge in clefts in the rocks and in caves. Tamsin often thought of her friend, and whenever she could, she accompanied her father on forays to look for him.

Over the next few months Simon was able to keep track of all the pangolins released on Phinda, thanks to their tags. All of the animals were regularly caught, weighed and checked and, of all of them, Zambezi did best. His placid and chilled nature had likely been an important factor in his survival.

By early 2020 a total of seven pangolins had been released by Simon. Two initially, then Zambezi's group of four, and then a little male that had been hand reared. Two of Zambezi's group did not make it. Simon lost track of one of them on a riverbank and then it just disappeared – it had possibly ended up in the river and drowned, or perhaps it had been eaten by a crocodile. Shortly after the pangolins' release it had rained heavily, and another of the four, unable to find a burrow to shelter in, had got very wet and very cold. It had to be returned to the veterinary hospital where they were not able to save it.

The five others, including Zambezi, continue to thrive. Their presence on Phinda, living wild and free, is a tribute to the diligence and bravery of Ray Jansen and the others involved in the sting rescue operations, the care of rehabilitation specialist Nicci, the veterinary professionalism of Dr Karin, and the hard work and dedication of Simon Naylor and the team at the reserve. The successful release of pangolins at Phinda is not only a conservation triumph, marking the reintroduction of a previously locally extinct species, it is also important on a symbolic level: the pangolins and their human helpers had won. For once in the story of the world's most trafficked wild mammal, the 'scales of injustice' had seen justice done.

Zambezi thrived, enjoying his regained freedom – but a clock was ticking in China. Midnight would soon strike, plunging the world into chaos. Humans would lose their freedom – and some, their life – due to a disease that might have connections to Zambezi's Asian cousins.

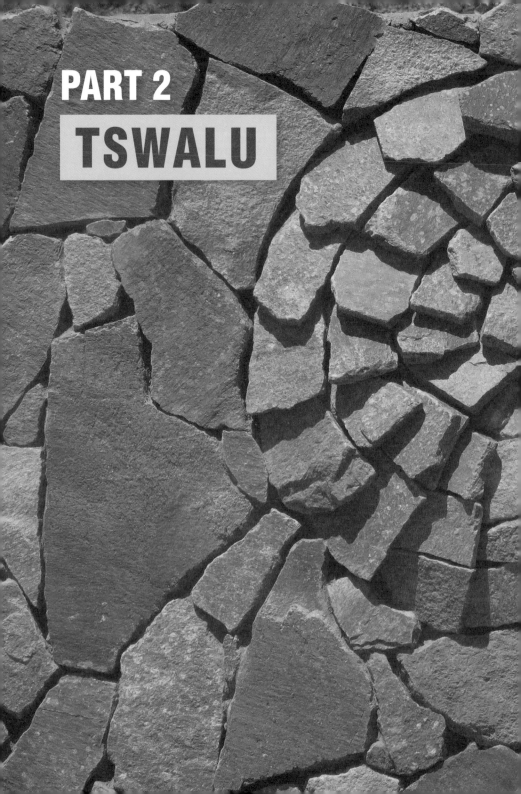

PART 2
TSWALU

Above: Wendy Panaino holds a telemetry aerial aloft on the
plains of Tswalu in order to locate tagged animals.
Previous spread: Clever stonework at Tswalu celebrates the pangolin,
one of the iconic species for which this reserve is world famous.

CHAPTER 8

A NEW BEGINNING

Tswalu Kalahari Reserve is the largest privately owned reserve in South Africa. Covering some 114,000 hectares, it lies in the southern Kalahari in South Africa's Northern Cape province, about 160 kilometres northeast of the town of Upington. *Tswalu* is a Setswana word meaning 'new beginning', and it is an appropriate name for a venture that has rescued the land from farming practices that destroyed much of the original fauna and flora.

The reserve was previously a collection of adjoining farms that were bought up by Stephen Boler, from the United Kingdom, and his German business partner Bill Schneider. Boler and Schneider had a vision: they wanted to give the area a new beginning by returning it to the pristine Kalahari dry savanna and the plants and animals that once lived there.

Their intention was to run the new reserve with income from responsible hunting, ecotourism, and by selling surplus animals. The area would be allowed to return to its original state and become a conservation model. Fences were removed and species that had been cleared by the farmers were reintroduced. The natural order of the entire area – which European settlers had many years earlier set about taming – was now reasserting itself.

Boler bought out his partner's shares, becoming Tswalu's sole owner, and was in the process of realising his African conservation ambitions when disaster struck in 1998. One day, as he was being flown in to the reserve's airstrip, he suffered a massive heart attack. The private aircraft instead headed for Johannesburg to get him to hospital as quickly as possible, but Stephen Boler didn't survive. This visionary founder of Tswalu didn't live to see his dreams fulfilled.

Not long before his untimely death, Boler had met Nicky Oppenheimer and his wife Strilli, to whom he had enthused about the Tswalu project.

Nevertheless, it was a surprise when, shortly after hearing that Boler had died, Nicky Oppenheimer received a phone call from Boler's lawyers saying that in his will, Boler had asked that the Oppenheimers be offered first refusal to buy Tswalu.

The Oppenheimers took over responsibility for the reserve and for continuing Stephen Boler's vision. Every day Tswalu brings the dream a little closer and fulfils the ambition of leaving the world, or at least a small part of it, in a better state than that in which it was found. In the words of Strilli Oppenheimer:

'Conservation of the environment, which we have inherited as custodians, is not only a subject of specialist and activist interest. It is an imperative for society to hand on a less distressed situation than we have caused. There is a growing public awareness in appreciating what we have, and in doing what we can together, to ensure we do not continue to lose species on a daily basis. Each loss impacts on everyone and everything in some way.'

Tswalu's new beginning was well under way, and one of the many creatures that benefited was the Temminck's pangolin, which helped place the reserve at the centre of pangolin research and ecotourism. Stephen Boler could scarcely have dreamt that, by 2019, the reserve he had helped establish would be known by nature lovers all over the world as one of the best places to view the world's most trafficked mammal.

Wendy Panaino is a scientist working at Tswalu. She works closely with Dylan Smith, one of the guides, who shares her enthusiasm for their work at Tswalu. And for sheer enthusiasm, Dylan is hard to beat. He refers to pangolins as 'the coolest craziest-looking animals', and although he often defers to Wendy on pangolin matters, he has plenty of his own stories. Shaking his head in wonder, he tells of a pangolin that was tagged in the north of the reserve and turned up, only two weeks later, right in the south, having walked 30 kilometres. Although Dylan has seen pangolins scent marking, he doesn't believe they physically defend territory from incursion by others, and has never observed any aggressive interactions.

He has seen lions playing with pangolins that have rolled into tight, armour-plated balls. Very often, the lion will paw the pangolin and roll it around, before getting bored and wandering off, leaving it alone. The only animal that Dylan is sure has taken pangolins on Tswalu is the honey badger. There is not a high density of honey badgers on the reserve, but there are recorded cases of pangolins being killed by them.

On a more sinister note, Dylan recalls how in 2017, in Kuruman, not far from Tswalu, he heard of a pangolin being offered for sale for what seemed to be a huge sum – a sum that would, however, by 2020, be regarded as a comparatively low price.

Wendy Panaino knows she is very lucky. She works in a wonderful place and does a job she loves. If she were offered the chance to trade her position and circumstances in life with anyone else she could think of, she wouldn't have to think long before saying 'No thank you!' Wendy is a full-time pangolin researcher based at Tswalu.

Like everyone else working for and with pangolins, she has become entranced and captivated by the enigmatic and compelling mammals that are the subject of her research. 'There is something magical about pangolins; I am getting goose bumps just talking about it. When you see them it just blows you away – they are unbelievable animals, everything about them, just special, special.'

When Wendy started her PhD through the University of the Witwatersrand (WITS) in 2015, while based at Tswalu, her focus of study was not specifically pangolins. Her main interest was in physiology and, in particular, how changes on the outside, such as temperature, affect what goes on inside a body. Temminck's pangolins were one of various animals under study, but as soon as she started dealing with this species, she fell in love with them.

Wendy Panaino

Dylan Smith

Pangolin tracks

Valery Phakaogo

'Scales of Injustice'

Pangolin skull

Finding out as much as possible about these animals became an obsession. How they live, and why they do what they do, were basic questions, which in turn gave rise to a host of other puzzles. She hoped that, once she had amassed a body of knowledge and understanding, she could play an effective role in their conservation.

The first pangolin she ever saw came walking straight towards her, and this initial contact became a defining moment. It was in winter 2015, in the middle of the day. 'I was looking for a particular tagged animal and was using tracking telemetry for the first time. I was totally lost in the dunes of Tswalu, and wrapped up in searching for the pangolin. We found the animal foraging at the base of a tree. It was the first time I had ever seen a pangolin. The tail was wrapped around the base of the tree, used as an anchor while he fed. I remember it as vividly as if it was yesterday. He got up and walked straight towards us. It was so surreal; this animal was not bothered by our presence, he was so relaxed he walked right up to us. He will always have a special place in my heart.'

While the formal, structured research Wendy is doing for her PhD forms the basis for her work, her general interest in everything about pangolins knows no bounds. She collects data on the size of typical foraging areas; to what degree they are nocturnal and/or diurnal – and the circumstances that influence this; the extent of their ranges; longevity; reproduction; distances travelled; types and depths of burrows, and a host of other issues. She is also monitoring factors that threaten the future of pangolins, such as trafficking by poachers, the erection of fences, farming practices and road mortality.

She has tracked pangolins and recorded data all over Tswalu. She has noted that individual pangolins have their own distinct personalities, and feels a deep empathy for them. For Wendy, poaching is not the only challenge pangolins face. The other great, looming danger for these animals, and for many other species, is climate change. As soon as her PhD is finished and published, she plans to make the potential impacts of climate change on pangolins and other species her major arena of study.

Wendy Panaino shares as much information as she can with visitors to Tswalu. Many of those coming to the reserve don't just want to see and photograph pangolins, they also want to learn about them, and they listen attentively as Wendy explains her work and discoveries. For instance, she explains that she is researching whether and to what degree the feeding patterns of the pangolins she is studying may have changed: for the first two years of her study the animals came out early in the day, then in the third year they came out at night. She concluded that differences in rainfall and the insect population appeared to influence foraging times – an opportune reminder of the subtle impact of climate change on the natural world.

Pangolins don't just feed on any ants and termites; they can be fussy about what species they go for. The cocktail ant gets its name because it cocks its tail when under threat, and this ant is a pangolin favourite. They commonly occur at the bases of trees, so out in the dunes where the trees are smaller – or absent – these favourite ants will probably not always be on the menu. On cleared farmland, where overgrazing has greatly reduced the occurrence of natural trees and grasses, ant and termite population densities will be low. So, to what degree are these areas able to sustain pangolins?

Their eyesight is relatively poor but pangolins have an extraordinary sense of smell. Even from a distance they are able to tell which trees are harbouring ant colonies in their bark, and which aren't. In this way, they select their tree and then peel away the bark. This not only exposes the ants, it agitates them too, and they come out in force – only to be met by the long sticky tongue of the feeding pangolin, repeatedly inserted and then withdrawn, covered in ants. Sticking your nose into ant and termite colonies inevitably leads to considerable irritation as the insects try to get into the predator's eyes, ears and nose. Pangolins restrict the entry of insects by constricting their nostrils, and their eyes have protective nictitating membranes as well as tough eyelids.

Cocktail ants, in particular, are tiny, and pangolins have to consume thousands during each feeding session – an estimated 20,000 ants may be taken by a single pangolin during a single feeding foray. But, as Wendy points out, pangolin research is still in its infancy, and she, too, is on a continuous journey of discovery. Finding the answers to the enormous number of unanswered questions is her driving force.

Wendy believes that climate change is potentially the 'elephant in the research room', and she plans a lot more research into its effect on pangolins and other species. 'There are lists everywhere of threats to pangolins: poaching, electric game fences, roadkill, farming, and other things, but climate change is rarely on the list. Records show that weather patterns are becoming more extreme and are predicted to become even more so. Foraging times appear to be influenced by temperature, and seem to change from being nocturnal in the summer to diurnal in the winter. If summers get hotter, pangolins' feeding habits might be compromised. It doesn't look good.

'I think pangolins probably can adapt; the question will be, can they adapt fast enough? Their reproductive rate, which is generally one pup a year, is not nearly high enough as a regeneration rate to inform genetic changes at a pace required to survive relatively fast-paced climate change. From generation to generation to generation the genes can adapt to new environments. Animals with high reproductive rates have much more chance of achieving the speed of genetic change required than animals like pangolins, with low reproductive rates. Quite simply, climate change appears to be happening too fast for many species. When environments change there are various options open to animals to change and adapt. They can adapt behaviourally by using more shade on hot days, by becoming more nocturnal or diurnal ... and by changing their diets. They can move to other areas with more favourable environments, but man-made barriers like fences nowadays often combine with natural barriers to inhibit movement.'

Wendy at work in the field, aerial in hand; sociable weaver nests adorn the thorn trees.

Technology has guided Wendy to a pangolin burrow.

Pangolins have a way of inveigling their way into people's lives. Valery Phakoago was born in a small rural village called Ga-Nchabeleng in Limpopo province. With the backing of her family, she studied hard and progressed through the ranks, achieving a distinction for her MSc in Environmental Sciences at the University of Venda.

In 2018, soon after she had started working as an intern in the Brain Function Research Group at WITS University, her mentor, Professor Andrea Fuller, offered her the opportunity of going to Tswalu to work with Wendy. Valery leapt at the chance but had no idea what she was in for. She arrived on the reserve in April, and any initial nervousness was dispelled by the open-hearted friendliness of everyone there. The excitement she felt that day, however, is still with her because Wendy introduced her to pangolins – an animal she had scarcely heard of and knew little about, but which would soon become central to her life.

She recalls, on seeing her first pangolin: 'As soon as I saw that animal I was amazed at this beautiful shy little animal. I got goose bumps I was so happy – I could hardly believe my eyes. I wondered how many people spend their whole lives without seeing one, or even knowing what it is. I fell in love with pangolins and I think they have changed my life.'

Like many before her, Valery had fallen under the spell of this enigmatic animal. She is now enrolled for a PhD, researching the dispersal of pangolin juveniles once they have left the care of their mother at four to six months old. Where do the juveniles go, how do they survive away from their mother, and how do they choose and establish their own home range? These are the questions that Valery – now commuting regularly between the university and Tswalu – is gearing up to answer.

Wendy and Valery hope their research will unlock some of the secrets of the pangolin, and contribute towards the conservation of the species. In early 2020, while these scientists immersed themselves in researching the behaviour, biology, physiology, reproduction and many other aspects of the Temminck's ground pangolin, their life and work – like the lives and work of others all over the world – was abruptly thrown into chaos by a new global pandemic: the latest coronavirus had arrived. The research work of other scientists, including virologists, was about to lift the lid on a shocking possibility – had the consumptive use of pangolins triggered the pandemic that would soon threaten every country on earth?

Although most visitors to the reserve realise that there can be no guarantees of seeing animals in the wild, because Tswalu is a world-renowned site for viewing pangolins, the guides are often under pressure to deliver sightings of these very discreet mammals. Knowing where the animals are and keeping an eye open for pangolin tracks have become essential tools in the daily jobs of the guides. Nevertheless, the guides often ask Wendy for help: she is in the field every day and has the technical means (telemetry) to track the animals.

Provided such viewing does not negatively impact on her research, Wendy is only too pleased to share her knowledge, and help the Tswalu guides find animals for their clients. People come back year after year to see the pangolins, which have surpassed other rare species like the aardwolf and the aardvark in the interest they generate.

It is impossible to spend time at Tswalu without falling under its spell, and feeling grateful for the 'new beginning' that Stephen Boler and Bill Schneider envisaged when they bought the farms and created the reserve. Tswalu has established an enviable reputation for its wildlife management, not least in connection with pangolins. The Oppenheimers' continued management of the reserve is based on sound conservation principles, and sustained by the belief that wilderness must be left wild, and in better condition than that in which it was found.

Those who work at Tswala, such as Wendy Panaino, Dylan Smith and Valery Phakoago, are aware that not only are they lucky to be working in such an environment, but also hugely privileged to be able to focus on the comings and goings of the amazing pangolin.

The research base at Tswalu

Dylan Smith

Lions, giraffes and gembok are all Tswalu residents.

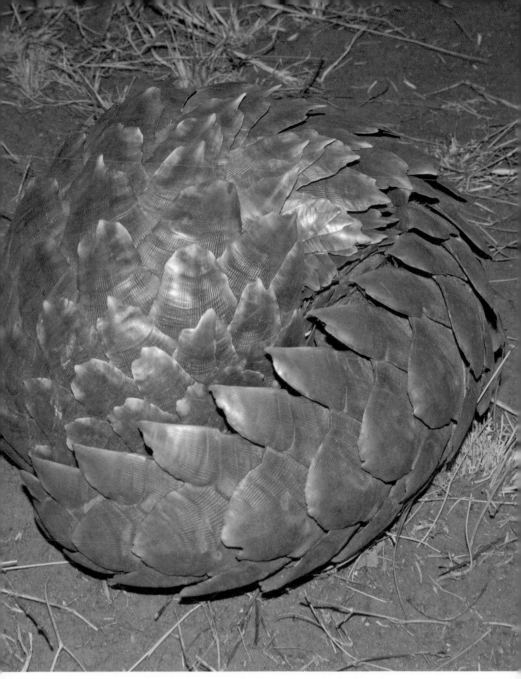

The ability to curl up and protect its soft underbelly
with sharp-edged overlapping scales has enabled the pangolin
to withstand attack, even from the mighty lion. (Dylan Smith)

CHAPTER 9
PANGOLIN TALES

Wendy Panaino has many personal stories to tell of her life as a pangolin researcher. 'In late 2015, early on in my pangolin-tracking career, I was learning about telemetry and deploying as many camera traps as I could. If we found an animal that was obviously pregnant, we just left it alone as far as telemetry was concerned, but did set camera traps. Saturday, 26th September 2015 was one of the most memorable days in my life studying pangolins; that was the first time I saw a baby pangolin, and my heart almost stopped. This was a huge moment. I had my laptop out in the field with me and was checking the footage from a camera trap, when there it was on the back of its mother – a baby pangolin about 15–18 centimetres (6 inches) long. I phoned everyone and told them "Oh my goodness we have a baby pangolin". I could tell from previous camera-trap footage that the baby was definitely less than a week old. It [was] an amazing sight, this little miniature pangolin riding along on its mother's back.'

She has, since this memorable day, seen other baby pangolins. The only likely chance of seeing a very young baby is when the mother is transferring it to another burrow – and then she is likely to take the quickest and shortest route possible. When the mother is out foraging the baby gets left behind in the burrow. At around three-and-a-half to four months, the baby starts coming out and foraging for itself. By 10 months at the latest, although they are still relatively small, young pangolins are completely independent.

'I have lots of pangolin pictures in my mind, but this first sight of a baby is one of my clearest memories. I don't "Disneyise" my pangolins and give them human names, but I do need to be able to separately identify them, and I remember that this mother was called P4, and the baby was P2.'

Wendy describes the events she experienced during a nightly vigil she was keeping at the burrow of a pangolin mother: 'I visited her most nights, monitoring her closely and checking the camera traps, and one night I was checking around her burrow when I heard her scratching, then she came out and her baby came out with her. They both investigated me, then the baby climbed onto her back and she started walking, and she walked, and walked, and walked. I followed her and walked until almost sunrise. She didn't stop; she went in a straight line, found a burrow and went down it. I had no idea where I was but I found my way back to my vehicle and later worked out that she had walked for almost three kilometres.'

One of the questions Wendy is often asked by Tswalu guests is 'Do the pangolins recognise you?' Although she doesn't know the answer for sure, there are compelling indications that they recognise her voice. 'On many occasions if I approach an animal slowly, quietly and carefully, and they don't know who I am, they go and find a bush to hide in, or roll into a ball, to wait for the potential threat to go. Then as soon as I say something, talk to them, they get up and walk off, foraging as they go. It's as if they know my voice, and think "Okay, it's just you, cool, I will carry on then".

'I know it sounds crazy but I do talk to them; at the end of a long day I sometimes ask them how their day has been, and how they are doing, and tell them how I have got on. Often, if I am in the field putting notes onto my laptop, I will tell them what I am doing and why. Sometimes they hear me talking on the phone, and sometimes I am with another person and they hear us talking. All the evidence points to their knowing and recognising my voice. It is kind of a cool thing to think they know and trust me, and are able to feel relaxed when I am with them.'

Wendy remembers a 76-year-old woman from California, whom she refers to as 'Hester', who had been hoping her entire life to see a pangolin. Individual visitors to Tswalu have their own personal guide, and their requests and desires are discussed with the guides – this personalises each guest's safari experience and enables many dreams to be fulfilled. Hester

Because pangolins are largely nocturnal, much of Wendy's work takes place at night.

Dylan Smith

Wendy Panaino

If Wendy were offered a chance to trade her position and circumstances in life with anyone else, she wouldn't have to think long before saying 'No thank you'.

had come to know about Tswalu and its high success rate of pangolin sightings, and had made the pilgrimage to fulfil a life-long quest.

Hester's requirement was simple: she wanted to see a live pangolin. More often than not, the game guides succeed in finding pangolins for their guests. In Hester's case, however, the best efforts of her guide were drawing blanks. Wendy got a call from the guide saying 'Please tell me you are out and are with a pangolin'. Hester's luck was in, but the pangolin Wendy was tracking was very shy, and she warned that it was therefore unlikely to be a great sighting.

The guide's vehicle pulled up a good distance away from the pangolin, and the expectant visitor got out, trembling with excitement. The pangolin was mostly obscured by a bush and all Hester saw was a tail. 'She turned around with tears streaming down her face and hugged me and said "I can't thank you enough for what you have done for me today." I apologised and told her I was so sorry it had not been a better sighting, but she was completely happy. She didn't want anything more and had realised her lifetime goal.' This experience with Hester once again underlined the magic and the power that pangolins hold for some people.

On another occasion an elderly American man visited the reserve. He was obviously very ill and was struggling to breathe. The impression was that he had pretty much risked his life to come to Tswalu. He was too sick to go on many game drives and stayed at the lodge most of the time. But he had come all the way to Africa just to see a pangolin, and Wendy sensed that once he had fulfilled this dream, he would be able to die a happy man – it was as simple as that.

The logistics were tricky as he was too short of breath to walk, and they would have to get him close enough to the subject for a viewing. They found a pangolin, but she was a nervous animal so they couldn't get too close. They watched her for a while through binoculars, and the old man was speechless with joy, just observing the little animal in her natural habitat. 'I was standing beside him and I could feel his emotion

In Tswalu's vastness, Wendy often helps the guides locate pangolins for visitors.

Dylan Smith

Storm clouds over Tswalu will bring rain that gives rise to new life.

as he watched his first pangolin – his face was transformed. He looked at peace, captivated by what he was watching, and he looked younger than he had before.

'Visitors to Tswalu keep thanking me when they see pangolins. It reminds me again how special this is for them.'

Wendy Panaino was finishing her PhD when I visited her at Tswalu. Once published, her paper will be available online.

PART 3

CHINA &
SOUTHEAST
ASIA

Above: The future of wildlife is in our hands.

(IISD/Kiara Worth (enb.iisd.org/cites/sc69/28nov.html))

Previous spread: Pangolins constrict their nostrils and ears and close
their eyes while eating in order to avoid being invaded by their prey. (Wendy Panaino)

CHAPTER 10

INEFFECTIVE AND IGNORED

CITES is the Convention on International Trade in Endangered Species. The convention text was drafted in 1963 following a resolution adopted at a meeting of the International Union for the Conservation of Nature (IUCN). The text of the resolution was finally accepted in Washington in March 1973 by 80 countries and, on 1st July 1975, the Convention came into force. CITES is an international agreement to which countries voluntarily subscribe, and its resolutions are legally binding on member states, which are known as Parties. CITES resolutions do not take the place of national laws, but each Party has to ensure that its domestic legislation reflects CITES resolutions and that they are implemented.

The organisation, which has its headquarters in Geneva, is often wrongly thought of as a conservation body. This is not the case – rather, it is an organisation that governs trade in order to avoid extinctions and protect threatened and vulnerable flora and fauna.

In 2020 there were 183 nation state signatories, plus the European Union which counts as a single party, making a total of 184 Parties to the Convention. Every two to three years there is a Conference of the Parties (COP), and threatened flora and fauna species are proposed for listings to regulate or stop international trade in them. Levels of trade are regulated and defined by listing on one of three appendices: Appendix I, II or III. Appendix I is for the most endangered animals and plants, which are threatened with extinction; all international trade is prohibited, unless for scientific research or in special circumstances. Appendix II allows specific controlled international trade that is monitored by CITES to ensure that the trade does not prove detrimental to the survival of the listed species in the wild. Appendix III is a list of species included at the request of a Party that already regulates trade in the species, but that needs the help and cooperation of other Parties to prevent unsustainable or illegal exploitation of the species.

Vietnam and Laos are two of the countries that import products from wild animal species – this in spite of the fact that under the CITES convention to which they have signed up, trading in many of those products is illegal.

During 2019 and 2020 several large shipments of pangolin scales that had originated in Nigeria were intercepted in Singapore. Experts believe these shipments could have accounted for over 100,000 African pangolins representing all four species. Some further believe that this figure may represent only about 10% of the total number being poached and illegally shipped to the Far East and China. Pangolins are a CITES Appendix I listed animal, so all commercial trade is banned.

The intercepted shipments indicated a huge illegal trade, and I wanted to see where this vast supply of pangolin products was ending up, and how easy it was for the consumer to buy pangolin scales, meat, and even live animals. My investigation took me to Hanoi, Hoa Binh, Vientiane and Ho Chi Minh City. To investigate the trade thoroughly would have taken months, not just the three weeks I had available, and I would have had to visit many more locations. Nevertheless, in my relatively brief excursion I discovered that pangolins, and a host of other illegal wildlife products from Africa and elsewhere, are freely on sale. What I witnessed made a complete mockery of those countries being Parties to CITES. It brought home to me just how toothless and meaningless international law can be if member countries decide to turn a blind eye and deliberately ignore the commitments they have made. In Vietnam and Laos the proof that CITES Appendix listings are ineffective and ignored was plain for all to see.

In her excellent book *Poached*, Rachel Love Nuwer describes the extent of the trade in illegal wildlife products in Vietnam, China and elsewhere in

The author in Hanoi on a mission investigating the trade in illegal wildlife ...

... and in a wet market

the Far East. During an extensive period of travel and research in these countries, her experience mirrored mine: illegal wildlife products were relatively easy to buy, international law was being ignored, and the trade in illegal products was never far away.

My investigation started in Hanoi in a rather obvious street in the tourist area called Lãn Ông Street, which is lined on both sides by shops selling traditional medicines and supplements for every type of ailment. I was working with colleagues Anton and Jasmine and an interpreter. We methodically made our way along both sides of the street. I had two main focuses: the first was to find tiger products, which could have originated from South Africa's lion bone supply, and the second was to check the availability of pangolin scales, meat and live animals.

Most of the shops in Lãn Ông Street were packed with legal products, and 'tiger balm' was obvious everywhere. There are two types of tiger balm: the legal ointment (a topical medication used to alleviate pain) and the illegal one, variously known as tiger balm, tiger cake and tiger glue. I was looking for the second type, which is derived from actual tiger body parts, including tiger bones.

Due to ever-increasing demand, and the fact that lion and tiger skeletons are almost impossible to tell apart, in recent years lion bones have been used to prepare tiger products, and in particular tiger cake and tiger wine. This market underpins South Africa's supply of lion bones to Southeast Asia. The bones are sourced from South Africa's captive lion breeding industry, and this is a highly profitable trade. In 2016, the CITES conference (COP17) was held in Johannesburg, and one outcome of it was that South Africa was given a special dispensation to export an annual quota of lion skeletons sourced from its captive breeding industry. The number of skeletons agreed for the first year's quota was 800.

A 15–18-kilogram lion or tiger skeleton is initially sold for about $1,500–$1,800. At an average of $1,650, the 800 carcasses in South Africa's 2017 quota were collectively worth $1,320,000 before processing. When boiled, a skeleton delivers about 60 portions (bars) of tiger or lion 'cake'. Of course, there are middlemen between the first seller and the final consumer; the processor, wholesaler and retailer all have profit margins and, in many cases, smugglers and others will have taken their cuts too. Each bar sells for $1,000, so each skeleton is worth $60,000 by the time it has been processed and sold to the end consumer as 'tiger cake'. This means the 800 skeletons were ultimately worth a staggering $48,000,000! Vietnam and China are the main consumer markets; other countries like Cambodia and Thailand are smaller consumers, and the size of the market in each country is heavily influenced by the size of its local Chinese and Vietnamese populations. In Vietnam, all tiger (lion) products are popular, but in China it is mostly tiger wine (a highly alcoholic beverage) that is in demand.

Tigers bred in Southeast Asia are used in the manufacture of traditional medicines and wine.

The author's research trip to Southeast Asia was a disappointing confirmation of what he had feared. (Pages 116–117: Jagged Peak Films)

Laos is a major entry port of illegal wild animal products for the entire region. According to the CITES trade database, Laos has a dominant position in the bone trade. Between 2009 and 2015 Laos bought over 2,000 complete skeletons from South Africa, and this figure excludes 2,300 bones and 40 skulls bought separately in the same period and sold as 'incomplete skeletons'.

We worked the street, and in every shop asked for tiger cake and pangolin. We were mostly met with negatives, head shaking, blank stares and sometimes were told these things could not be sold because they are illegal. However, in less than three hours we got lucky and were told we could buy 100 grams of tiger cake for $1,000. We were told that it wasn't in the shop, but if we wanted it we could collect it the next day. Pangolin scales could also be supplied if required.

We pretended interest in the tiger cake and Anton and I went back the next night. We were expecting a covert drug-dealing type of situation, and were worried that things might get difficult and dangerous when we made our excuses not to buy. Jasmine and our interpreter/guide were not with us, but were serving as backup if needed. We agreed on cell phone messages and various actions they could take if we signalled we were in trouble.

In the end our worries proved to be unfounded and our precautions unnecessary. The shop had an open front and the counter was almost on the street. As soon as we arrived a bar of chocolate-like substance was produced and placed on the counter for our inspection. I surreptitiously picked it up and examined it while using my body to shield it from being seen by anyone in the street. I then handed it back under the counter. The man I handed it to once again placed it in plain view on the counter!

We were allegedly buying the tiger cake for a friend in Hong Kong, and told the seller that, now that we had seen it, we would report to our friend and get back to him. I also again mentioned that I would let them know if we needed pangolin scales. We then left and headed for a bar – to discuss and analyse our experience while the details were still fresh in our minds.

We had both been struck by the relaxed and open attitude that the seller had when dealing in an illegal product. That the product was illegal was widely acknowledged, but this didn't lead to any particular caution when trading in it. With no special introductions and within only a few hours of starting open enquiries in normal shops, I had been shown tiger cake and offered pangolin scales.

In addition to our interpreter, we had a driver, who had somehow realised that we were shopping for 'under-the-counter' substances. He knew of a traditional medicine dealer in Hoa Binh who could provide tiger cake. With the driver and interpreter, we set off the next day for Hoa Binh, which is some three hours from Hanoi. On arrival at the dealer's house we were greeted by a charming elderly couple who gave us tea and refreshments, and then a briefcase was produced which was full of bars of tiger cake. There was clearly a standard price because once again 100 grams would cost $1,000. This was proving depressingly and ludicrously easy. We had no special 'ins', were only on our third day, and were having no trouble sourcing pangolin and tiger products, both of which are CITES Appendix I listed animals. This illegal dealing in wildlife products was going on right under the noses of the authorities.

Our next stop was Vientiane, the capital of Laos where, if anything, our quest became more bizarre and even easier. We visited the San Jiang market near the airport, and almost immediately found ourselves in a situation bordering on ludicrous. Surrounding the San Jiang hotel and other hotels were shops, and in window displays and under glass-topped counters, totally open to view, were pangolin scales, pangolin wine, tiger (or possibly lion) wine, tiger bone carvings, tiger teeth and claw jewellery, ivory, rhino horn, and even a tiger whip, which looked like a bloody skinned tiger tail. The shop assistants were not remotely embarrassed or shy about discussing any of the products, none of which, according to international law, should have been on sale. If we could see pangolin scales, tiger wine and other illegal products openly on sale in shops, so could the police – yet where were they?

Most of the shop assistants appeared to be Chinese. So technically, just like us, they were foreign guests in another country. Foreign guests they may have been, but their couldn't-care-less, almost arrogant demeanour strongly indicated that they knew they had nothing to fear from the law of the country in which they were guests.

After San Jiang, our guide took us to the Packchum and Donmachey live animal markets. He had told us that the legal animals were on open display, while the illegal ones were hidden under the tables. The range of animal species available for sale was quite astonishing: toads, frogs, dogs, cats, piglets, pigeons, snakes, various fish, rabbits, scorpions, rats, mice, chickens, a huge variety of small birds, various small mammals, bats, bugs and cockroaches, shellfish, a large bear, monkeys and almost anything else one could imagine.

Almost as soon as Anton, Jasmine, our guide and I started walking along the rows of tables and among the cages, the atmosphere became charged with suspicion. Whether they were suspicious of westerners in general, worried that we might be a documentary film crew, or connected to the police, I don't know. The atmosphere was anything but relaxed, and clearly there would have been no point in asking for any of the illegal exotic species that we suspected were hidden in crates under the tables.

Although we were not able to witness the same brazen selling of illegal products that we had seen in San Jiang, these 'wet' markets were horrifying examples of the culture prevalent in the Far East, in which literally anything and everything from the animal world, alive or dead, both wild and domestic, is eaten. In Zimbabwe, poverty had driven Joseph to poach a pangolin. In the Far East, too, poverty is certainly a major driver behind what is eaten: when you are starving you will eat anything. The 'eat-anything' end of the spectrum might apply to what was on sale on the tables in the markets. It would not apply to the expensive, exotic luxury items probably hidden under the tables, but so openly on sale in the shops in San Jiang.

After Vientiane we returned to Vietnam, where our final stop was Ho Chi Minh City, formerly known as Saigon. We had only two full days in the city so had to be careful with our time. It may be that we just struck it lucky, but in Ho Chi Minh City the trading of illegal wildlife was even easier to find than it had been in Hanoi or Vientiane.

In her book *Poached*, Nuwer lists various restaurants in Ho Chi Minh City that serve 'exotics' such as pangolins. We randomly selected a restaurant called Huong Rung. I asked if they had anything special on the menu, like wild meat. We had walked in off the street, once again had no special introduction, and could easily have been members of law enforcement. With no suspicion, and without batting an eyelid, the head waiter said that he had civet immediately available. This was a staggering response for various reasons, but chief among them was that civets are often cited as having been one of the probable vectors, or disease-carrying interfaces, for the Severe Acute Respiratory Syndrome (SARS) virus on its way to humans.

SARS was a deadly disease outbreak that began in Guangdong in China in 2002. It was a strain of coronavirus usually found in bats and other small animals. The outbreak took over a year to bring under complete control, and was mostly restricted to China and other Southeast Asian countries, although there was a significant outbreak in Toronto in Canada. By the time the outbreak had petered out, there had been over 8,000 cases reported, and nearly 800 deaths. This 10% death rate ranked SARS high on the list of deadly diseases, and in response to the outbreak, the Chinese government temporarily suspended trade in wildlife products, including civets. This ban was later relaxed and 17 years later another deadly coronavirus, called Covid-19, would emerge, with wild animals once again almost certainly being the source of the virus. And here I was, standing in a restaurant in Vietnam's second city, being offered the chief SARS vector suspect for lunch! Civets are not considered an endangered species, but they can certainly be considered a species that was highly likely to have caused hundreds of deaths, endangered thousands more human lives, and led to severe economic damage.

Being offered civet for lunch was only the start. I told the waiter, who had an air of authority about him and might have been the owner, that I had eaten civet and was hoping for something different. I asked him if he could make pangolin available. In the blink of an eye he said yes, I could have pangolin meat at 7,000,000 Dong per kilogram. I calculated this in front of him, and it came to $300 per kilogram. Maybe he thought I considered this too expensive, because next he offered me a whole animal for $4,000. I said that, in view of not knowing which pangolin species he was offering, and therefore what it would likely weigh, I thought this was expensive; but he was happy to negotiate, and – in three steps – I bargained him down to a price of $3,000. He obviously thought I was a serious potential buyer, because he then took me upstairs to a large dining room, and showed me a private room just off it, with a table laid for 10 people. He said that the price of the private dining room would be included in the price of the pangolin, along with the rest of the dinner. I said I would have to think about it, and he obviously thought I was doubting I would get genuine pangolin, so he said he would bring the pangolin to show me before dinner. The clear implication was that, if it would convince me, they would bring the animal and kill it in front of me to prove that I was getting what I was paying for. In the space of 15 minutes in one restaurant, I had been offered both of the animals that are conceivably the vectors for SARS-1 and SARS-2 (Covid-19).

Our guide also took us to an old part of the city that was home to several traditional medicine shops. In two shops I was offered pangolin scales (which still had flesh attached) in sealed clear plastic envelopes; and in a third shop I was told that I could have pangolin scales if I came back in an hour.

In a nearby shopping centre that extended over three floors, a lot of the shops were selling handicrafts. Ivory, tiger claws, bear claws, carved tiger (maybe lion) bone trinkets, pangolin scales and other illegal wildlife products were all openly on sale in several places.

One got the impression that both Vietnam and Laos were vast illegal wildlife supermarkets. But they are dwarfed by neighbouring China which, with its 1.4 billion people, is the largest consumer on earth of wildlife products, both legal and illegal.

Consumption of products from the natural world is deep-rooted in many Eastern cultures: traditional medicine and eat-anything poverty are two major drivers at one end of the consumer hierarchy; luxury food consumption, recreational use and status are at the other.

From a medical science perspective, the consumption by humans of products from wild animal species can be very dangerous. Pathogens are microscopic organisms that can cause disease, and medical scientists have been concerned for many years about pathogens that can be found in wild animals infecting humans.

AIDS (thought to have first crossed from chimps to humans about 100 years ago), bird flu, swine flu, Ebola (first identified in 1976), SARS and Middle East Respiratory Syndrome (MERS) are all potentially deadly viruses that have crossed from animals to humans.

It is stunningly irresponsible that, with over 100 years of evidence that animals can be vectors for viruses deadly to humans, China and other Far Eastern countries have not listened and learnt. During my trip to Vietnam and Laos I had been offered snake wine, snake bile wine, cobra flesh, pangolin meat, tiger cake, civet and much else. With their burgeoning trade in, and consumption of, wildlife products, which carry pathogens that can prove fatal to humans, these communities are placing themselves and the rest of the world at risk.

In late 2019 the world's latest coronavirus, Covid-19, first reared its head in China; and it would go on to infect the whole world, kill hundreds of thousands, and cause unprecedented economic upheaval. China and the Far East are the consumers, but it takes two hands to clap, and the main source of wildlife is Africa. Starting with AIDS 100 years ago, and progressing through all the other animal-borne viruses, we have had ample warning. We have not listened and are now paying a terrible price.

A range of wild animals is caught and imprisoned in small cages to be sold at wet markets across Southeast Asia. (Dan Bennett / CC BY 2.0)

CHAPTER 11

CHINA'S VIRUS?

'IT CAME FROM CHINA' – PRESIDENT DONALD TRUMP

(I would like to thank professor Ray Jansen
for his help and advice with this chapter.)

Covid-19 is one of seven coronaviruses known to infect humans. The others are SARS-CoV, MERS-CoV, HKUI, NL63, OC43 and 229E, with the latter four being associated with milder symptoms.

In the 17 years between the first SARS outbreak in 2002 and the appearance of the novel coronavirus (Covid-19) at the end of 2019, the consumption of wildlife, particularly African wildlife, by China and other Far Eastern countries has increased year on year. Many species of animal are prized for their meat and/or other body parts, including iconic tigers, lions, rhinos and elephants, along with many smaller creatures, and, increasingly, pangolins. Some are locally bred, but most are poached and trafficked in order to cater for the seemingly insatiable, ever-expanding consumer markets. In the last chapter I described my visit to two countries that were ignoring international law and were, in effect, wildlife supermarkets for whole animals and body parts, most of which were being sold illegally. As consumption has increased so has the risk, and finally the consequences are upon us, bringing human life on earth to its knees.

I was in Tswalu on 8th February 2020 when Barry Lovegrove, a fellow Struik Nature (Penguin Random House) author who knew I was writing a book on pangolins, approached me, carrying his laptop. He was coming to tell me the breaking news that scientists believed that pangolins were the likely carriers of Covid-19 to humans.

Wendy Panaino, a research scientist stationed at Tswalu, is a globally acknowledged pangolin expert, and it didn't take long for the world's

Over 97 tonnes of illegally shipped scales from Africa were intercepted being exported into Asia in 2019. This equates to some 160,000 pangolin victims – and many more tonnes probably evaded detection.

Wendy Panaino

media to find her, and emails from major broadcasters and newspapers from all over the world to come flooding in. The African Pangolin Working Group and others were similarly inundated with requests for information – on a species that most people in the world had never even heard of.

Some viruses can be transmitted directly to humans from bats, birds and other hosts. However, this transmission process more often involves an intermediary or vector. The host is sometimes referred to by virologists and epidemiologists as a reservoir species, and on its way to humans from the reservoir species and through the vector, the virus may combine with another virus in a process called a recombination, or it may mutate. In either event, a more deadly virus may result.

Wet markets in China and other Southeast Asian countries are market places selling fresh meat. Cages containing birds, bats and many other small mammals are often stacked on top of each other. Urine and faeces drop down through the cages onto the animals stacked below; thus, if bats are stacked in cages above civets or pangolins, those animals can end up taking in body fluids from the bats above them. A bat coronavirus genome is 96% similar to the human version, while pangolin coronavirus is 90% similar. Chinese scientists further discovered that the S-protein in Covid-19 is 97.4% similar to the S-protein found in bats. This strongly indicates bats as being the reservoir species.

An RBD is a 'receptor binding domain', an area in the stalks of the virus, and it is here that some of the deadliest characteristics of the virus are hidden. The RBD and its amino acids are a 96% match in both pangolin and human coronaviruses. This does not prove that pangolins are the Covid-19 infection agent, but it is a compelling signpost.

A paper by four Chinese scientists (from Hainan, Fujian and Central South Universities and a laboratory) says that Covid-19 almost certainly recombined in pangolins before making the jump to humans. They believe that bats were the reservoir species, pangolins the vector, and humans (via China's wet markets) the recipients – that Covid-19 is very possibly a recombination of bat and pangolin coronaviruses.

The work of Chinese researchers was in line with that of American scientists from the Baylor College of Medicine in Texas. The US research identified the Malayan pangolin as the likely vector. Researcher Matthew Wong from Baylor College discovered that the distinctive RBD docking mechanism in Covid-19 was identical to that found in the Malayan pangolin coronavirus. Professor Joseph Petrosino, Wong's Baylor College supervisor, said that pangolin and bat viruses may have come together in the same animal, and recombined with devastating results, creating the novel coronavirus.

In a letter to *Nature Medicine* published on 17th March 2020, research scientists Kristian Andersen, Andrew Rambaut and Robert Garry make clear their opinion that Covid-19 is not a laboratory construct or a purposefully manipulated virus. Their letter discusses the Malayan pangolin as being involved as a probable vector. Research performed largely by scientists associated with the University of Michigan joins the ever-growing body of scientific opinion favouring Malayan pangolins as the link for infection between bats and humans. This work torpedoes earlier theories that snakes may have been the vector. In addition, it disproves another theory associating Covid-19 with the virus that causes HIV AIDS.

In a prescient scientific article published in the journal *Clinical Microbiology Reviews* in October 2007, the authors, led by Vincent Cheng, state in their concluding paragraph that 'the presence of a large reservoir of SARS-CoV-like viruses in horseshoe bats, together with the culture of eating exotic mammals in southern China, is a time bomb. The possibility of the re-emergence of SARS and other novel viruses from animals or laboratories and therefore the need for preparedness should not be ignored.' The world ignored this and countless other warnings and 12 years later the time bomb exploded in the form of Covid-19.

Scientists are cautious until they are certain, and until the science has been peer reviewed and accepted as proven, the 'Covid-19 to humans via bats and pangolins' claim cannot be taken as fact. Professor Petrosino did make the following statement: 'A virus known to exist in bats, and a virus found in a pangolin virus sample appear to have recombined to form SARS-CoV 2 (Covid-19). But some viruses can be transmitted between mammals relatively easily, so there is no way to tell whether there is another animal where these two viruses perhaps co-existed. More surveillance is necessary.'

There have been challenges to these pangolin theories, but several other studies also explored the link, and the majority of scientific opinion supports the likelihood of pangolins being the Covid-19 vector. It is worth noting that in the 17 years since the SARS outbreak in 2002, scientists have still not reached 100% agreement as to how that virus got to humans.

Before the end of December 2019, US officials were already pressing China for more data about the disease, and for the opportunity to work directly with virologists in Wuhan. China's reluctance to grant access to data and to Wuhan's scientists did nothing to calm the suspicion and rumours that accompanied the growing pandemic. As the virus spread during April and May 2020, so did the war of words between the United States and China.

In early May, a headline from *The Times* (UK) read: 'I've seen evidence that it came from Chinese lab, says Trump'. A similar approach was adopted by his Secretary of State and other senior US officials, although no actual proof or evidence was offered to back up this position, and top US officials have subsequently backed off from this allegation. Early on in the blame game, a Chinese official claimed that the virus had been brought to Wuhan by American athletes taking part in international military games. In addition to the US/Chinese claims and counterclaims, there was a bewildering array of conspiracy theories, amongst which was the idea that the virus had been engineered by China to destabilise Western economies, and that 5G technology had played a part in the outbreak.

With its enormous population, giant cities, huge trade in wildlife, and its wet markets, China is a vast viral petri dish. After the outbreak of SARS in 2002, and again after Avian influenza A (H7N9) in 2013, the Chinese government acted to close wet markets in the country. Yet these efforts were half-hearted and shockingly short-lived and within months the markets were up and running again. Early in 2020, with Covid-19 ravaging almost every country in the world and bringing the global economy to its knees, was a replay unfolding?

Chinese government moves in January and February 2020 to ban and limit trade and consumption of terrestrial wildlife products were a little late. The stable door was being closed after the horse had bolted. Or was it being closed? On Sunday, 6th April 2020, the UK's mass circulation tabloid newspaper, the *Daily Mail*, published an article in their *Mail Online* edition saying that China's wet markets were once again open and operating as they always had. As I had witnessed in Vientiane in Laos, these markets sell an extraordinary variety of both wild and domestic animals. Exposed bloody meat can easily become infected, and there is no provision for even basic hygiene, with different animals being slaughtered and skinned on the same surfaces without any proper cleaning in between. The newspaper was reporting from a market in Guilin in southwest China, and another correspondent photographed a medicine seller re-opening his business in Dongguan selling bats and other animals. The *Daily Mail*'s correspondent in Dongguan was quoted as saying, 'The markets have gone back to operating in exactly the same way as they did before the coronavirus. The only difference is that security guards now try to stop anyone taking pictures, which would never have happened before.'

From January 2020 onwards there was considerable reporting, in both mainstream and social media platforms, of modifications to China's Wildlife Protection Law (WPL). Much of the published information was misleading or inaccurate. The first development came on 26th January, when three Chinese agencies, the Ministry of Agriculture and Rural

Affairs, the National Forestry and Grasslands Administration, and the State Administration for Market Regulation issued the 'Notification regarding the prohibition of trade in wildlife'. This required all facilities keeping wild animals in captivity to quarantine them; and all consumptive operators, including food outlets, supermarkets and produce markets, were banned from selling wild animals in any form. The ban was to last until the national coronavirus epidemic was over. There appeared to be grey areas in the ban, such as the status of products sold for Traditional Chinese Medicine (TCM), and manufactured products such as tiger or lion bone, wine and cake.

On 24th February 2020, China's highest law-making body, the National People's Congress (NPC), put in place a series of measures that appeared to back up and strengthen the restrictions imposed in January. These measures prohibited trade in most terrestrial wild animal species consumed as food. The ban only covered food, so trade in pets, TCM and ornamental artifacts was not addressed. Although there seemed to be notable loopholes, which meant the measures fell short of being a total ban, these moves indicated significant departures from the existing WPL, and seemed to demonstrate recognition of the dangers posed by wildlife consumption. Although the pandemic had triggered moves by China's lawmakers, many issues needed to be reviewed and resolved before permanent changes could be made to the WPL. The term 'wildlife' would need to be defined, in terms of whether it covered captive-bred species. Some items used in TCM, such as pangolin scales, might still be able to be traded and consumed if classed as TCM – although this would fly in the face of the ban on commercial trade in all eight pangolin species, which are CITES Appendix I listed, whether TCM or not. One way sellers explain the trade in pangolin scales is by claiming that the scales are part of stockpiles that pre-dated pangolins being Appendix I listed (see STOP PRESS on pages 158–159).

It was also announced that the WPL would be revised during 2020 and a review process started. Pro-wildlife campaigners and conservationists hope the amendments will result in a permanent ban on all trade in wildlife, and that the ban will be enforced. Those hoping for such a ban are concerned that items used in TCM will escape restriction, as may

中华人民共和国第十二届全国人民代表大会第一次会议

Following the global Covid-19 outbreak, China's National People's Congress undertook a review of the country's wildlife trade and consumption laws.

captive-bred wild animals. They argue that such exemptions would create loopholes for opportunists, which would seriously compromise the effectiveness of the new amendments. One encouraging indicator is a proposal to buy out or compensate wildlife farmers who agree to switch to alternative forms of 'agriculture'.

The NPC meeting in May passed new laws affecting Hong Kong, but revision of the WPL did not come up. At the time of this book's going to print in early October 2020 the review process was ongoing, and people worldwide were waiting to find out what new measures would eventually become law. The coronavirus pandemic has left the world in no doubt that China's wildlife laws affect every human living on the planet.

The value of the trade in wild animal products in China in 2019 was estimated to be over $70 million, which is a huge sum. In contrast it is thought that the first SARS epidemic in 2003 probably cost the world's economy around $50 billion, and some believe that this second SARS pandemic could result in a loss of $25–30 trillion, leading to a deep recession and, quite possibly, a depression. The economic devastation will probably cause as much death and misery as the medical pandemic. The eating habits of one set of cultures will represent the most expensive meals in the history of the human race.

The World Health Organisation's International Health Regulations (2005) are a legally binding instrument of international law that aims to (a) assist countries to work together to save lives and livelihoods endangered by the international spread of diseases and other health risks, and (b) avoid unnecessary interference with international trade

Wildlife sold in Southeast Asia's wet markets is suspected of having caused the SARS-1 outbreak in 2002/2003, and the 2019/2020 Covid-19 pandemic.

and travel. The signatories include China and the other Far Eastern wildlife-eating countries. It seems that, by failing to learn the lessons of the dangers posed to human health by consuming wild animal products, these countries are ignoring their responsibilities under international law.

If science does eventually conclude, emphatically, that Covid-19 came to humans via the illegal sale of pangolins in Wuhan's wet markets, then China stands guilty before the world. The Communist Party's situation was further compromised by their choosing to silence the early warnings about the latest virus, tragically illustrated by the death of a medical doctor, Li Wenliang, whose attempt at whistle-blowing was brutally suppressed. Professor Steve Tang, director of the SOAS China Institute in London, was quoted in the UK press in April 2020: 'In terms of priority [in China], controlling the narrative is more important than the public health or the economic fallout. It doesn't mean the economy and public health are not important. But the narrative is paramount.' According to western press reports, such as appeared in *The Observer* (UK) on 12th April 2020, documents relating to research and publishing procedures published online by Chinese universities appeared and were then quickly removed.

China has questions to answer. Did the virus originate from the 'wet' markets, or from lax practices at the Wuhan research centre? Furthermore, why are sensitive and potentially dangerous research establishments located in a major city, and not in an isolated rural area? Between 12th and 31st December there were at least 104 Covid-19 cases and 15 deaths in Wuhan, yet at the end of the month the Chinese government's official line was still that there was no clear evidence of human-to-human transmission of the virus! The province of Hubei was sealed off from the rest of China early in the outbreak, but not from the rest of the world. Why?

If China and the Far East stop consuming, then Africa and others will stop supplying. Wildlife will benefit hugely, and mankind will have pressed one of the many re-set buttons that the Covid-19 lesson invites us to do.

PART 4
SCALES OF INJUSTICE

Above: Where food is scarce, people are driven to consume
whatever edible species are available. (African Pangolin Working Group)
Previous spread: Pangolins often fall victim to Central
and West Africa's bushmeat trade. (African Pangolin Working Group)

CHAPTER 12

BIOLOGY, HISTORY AND SYMBOLISM

There are eight pangolin species in the world; four are found in Africa, and four in Asia.

AFRICAN PANGOLIN SPECIES

The **Temminck's ground pangolin** (*Smutsia temminckii*) occurs widely but is found mostly in southern and East Africa. This is a medium-sized pangolin with a body weight of around 9–11 kilograms, and a total length (including the tail) of up to 140 centimetres. However, significant regional size and weight variations have been noted; for example, pangolins found in the Kalahari are smaller and lighter than animals from elsewhere in the range. And in Sudan there is a record from 1974 of a male weighing 21 kilograms, which is double the average weight for the species. Temminck's pangolins are widely distributed in savanna, flood plain and woodland areas throughout their southern and East African range.

Unlike other pangolin species, the Temminck's pangolin is bipedal, walking only on its hind legs. It holds its long tail parallel to the ground, so that it acts as a counterweight, enabling the pangolin to hold its short front legs off the ground and not use them when moving. The animal's back and sides are covered with some 400 scales which, together with the skin, make up 33–35% of the animal's total weight. Scales from this and other pangolin species are, like rhino horn, composed of keratin. They are much sought after in China and the Far East, where they are ground down for use in medicine.

Although they themselves are, to a limited extent, preyed on by other animal species, by far the main threat to this pangolin is from human actions and influences, with poaching, roadkill, electrocution on electric fences, habitat degradation and other factors all taking their toll.

The Temminck's pangolin is listed as Vulnerable on the IUCN Red List.

The **Giant pangolin** (*Smutsia gigantea*) is the largest of all eight pangolin species, and occurs in Equatorial Africa. The total body length is 140–180 centimetres, and their weight varies from 30–40 kilograms. In some respects, they are similar to their cousins, the Temminck's pangolin, but they have relatively larger forelimbs, are not bipedal, have a less rounded tail and have more scales; and they do more digging. They are mostly nocturnal and do not appear to have a specific breeding season.

As with Temminck's pangolins and all other species, their main threat is from humans. Hunting and poaching for bushmeat and traditional medicine for the local market, as well as, increasingly, for trafficking to China and the Far East, is unsustainable and could lead to local extinctions.

The Giant pangolin is listed as Endangered on the IUCN Red List.

The **White-bellied pangolin** (*Phataginus tricuspis*) is native to West and Central Africa and is found mostly in lowland tropical forests and secondary forests. It is a small pangolin, weighing only 1–3 kilograms, and reaching a total length of about 100 centimetres.

This species is semi-arboreal (lives in trees) and has 794–1,141 scales. The forelegs are slightly shorter than the hind legs and all four limbs are used in climbing and walking. Like the Giant and Temminck's pangolins, this species is primarily nocturnal. It spends time both on the ground and in trees, and passes most of the day in tree hollows or in the forks of branches. Habitat degradation and destruction, as well as over-exploitation by humans, are once again the main threats.

The White-bellied pangolin is listed as Endangered on the IUCN Red List.

The **Black-bellied pangolin** (*Phataginus tetradactyla*) is arboreal and very similar in size and weight to the White-bellied pangolin, albeit with a slightly longer body of around 120 centimetres. The Black-bellied species gets its name from the black skin that covers most of its ventral (under) side. The rest of the pangolin is covered in scales numbering 542–637. It is found in West and Central West Africa, and has been less studied than the other species. Once again, the main threats are from humans. Although the species is protected by legislation in its range countries, law enforcement is ineffective.

The Black-bellied pangolin is listed as Vulnerable on the IUCN Red List.

The four Asian pangolin species are the **Chinese pangolin** (*Manis pentadactyla*); the **Indian pangolin** (*Manis crassicaudata*); the **Sunda pangolin**, also known as the **Malayan** or **Javan pangolin** (*Manis javanica*); and the **Philippine pangolin** (*Manis culionensis*)

Wild species all over Africa have places and functions in the lives of humans, although few mammals can compete with the continents' four pangolin species in the many ways in which they influence the lives of indigenous African peoples. Throughout their ranges, from north to south, from east to west, African pangolins have particular significance for their human neighbours, and play a special part in the lives of tribes and individuals.

In his Foreword at the beginning of this book, Bushman elder Izak Kruiper told of some of the ways that pangolins have special symbolism and importance for Bushmen. Many other tribes also regard them as sacred, and pangolins have special places in the cultures of many African peoples.

The Lele (or Leele) tribe live on the western bank of the Kasai River in what is now the Democratic Republic of the Congo (DRC), although in recent years many have migrated to Kinshasa. In the late 1940s and early 1950s, anthropologist Mary Douglas studied a Lele cult, the members of which were called 'Pangolin Men'. Various attributes qualified village men to become initiates into the cult. Aspiring cult members had to have produced both a male and a female child from the same wife, and both the aspirant and his wife had to be from the village's founding families. In addition, the candidate had to have killed and eaten a pangolin as part of the initiation ceremony. Once initiated, Pangolin Men were invested with powerful hunting and fertility prowess. They, along with their wives, were responsible for moving the village to new locations from time to time. When a new village was established, the Pangolin Man and his wife had to be the first to sleep on the new ground.

Douglas witnessed various other pangolin-linked rites among the Lele, including occasions when pangolins were killed and eaten to promote successful hunts. Killing pangolins was not done lightly, and villagers expressed shame and embarrassment at having killed and eaten the animal unless it had been done for ritual purposes. The Lele perceived pangolins to be almost supernatural, describing them as being fish-like – an allusion to their covering of scales. Pangolins were believed to be connected to the spirits that control human fertility, and women were not allowed to touch them.

By the time Mary Douglas revisited the Lele in 1988, Christianity had spread throughout the region and the pangolin cult had been outlawed.

Various other Bantu-speaking ethnic groups in and around the rainforest regarded the pangolin as having special symbolism and significance. In Bembe cosmology, the pangolin has special cultural significance, and is viewed as a mediator between the worlds of the living and the dead. The species is associated with death because it is nocturnal, lives underground, and feeds on termites, which are associated with corpses. It is said that women learnt how to carry their babies on their back by observing pangolins, and copied the overlapping effect of scales when roofing their houses.

The Lega are northern neighbours of the Bembe and, like the Bembe, believe that the pangolin's overlapping scales inspired their method of house construction. Among the Lega it is forbidden to kill pangolins, and if a pangolin is found dead, the Lega perform various rituals to purify themselves individually, and cleanse the community.

Among the Hamba from the north of Kasai Province in the DRC, the killing of Giant pangolins is generally forbidden. However, a relatively new political institution, the 'Masters of the Forest', may eat pangolin meat. This is a closed male brotherhood practising secret rites that are off limits to women and those who are not members of the brotherhood. If a pangolin is trapped by a non-member, a heavy fine must be paid to the Masters of the Forest.

The Tabwa, who live at the southwestern end of Lake Tanganyika, believe that the king of beasts is not the lion but the pangolin, because of its formidable armour and other unusual qualities.

The pangolin is also of importance in some West African cultures, and the Gogo, who live in the Côte d'Ivoire, link pangolins to both war and fertility. The Sangu of southern Tanzania believe that pangolins fall from the sky, having been sent to earth by the tribe's ancestors. In various cultures, and for different rites and rituals, pangolins are dressed in black cloth. Many of these tribes regard encounters with pangolins as special events that should be followed up with specific rituals. It is generally held that the animals should not be killed. Scales and other body parts should only be taken from pangolins that have died naturally, or been sacrificed as part of rituals.

Among the Lovedu of Limpopo province in South Africa, Temminck's pangolins traditionally belong to their Queen, and as with the Kalahari Bushmen, they believe pangolins have a role in bringing rain. To the north, in Zimbabwe, the Shona were forbidden to kill pangolins, and if someone transgressed, they would provoke the anger of their ancestors and incur material penalties.

In Asia, too, the four pangolin species often have special significance among indigenous peoples. Pangolins are regarded as sacred and are deified in some cultures; killing them is generally believed to be wrong and to bring penalties.

If pangolins are proved to be the vector to humans of the SARS virus that produced Covid-19, there are many people in many cultures who would agree with Bushman Izak Kruiper that punishment visits those who abuse these animals.

Law enforcement fights a daily battle to catch those involved in trafficking pangolins and their scales. (Will Clothier)

CHAPTER 13

'MOST TRAFFICKED MAMMAL IN THE WORLD'

The pangolin's claim to fame as the world's most trafficked wild mammal is not an achievement that any species would aspire to. In the last few years people have increasingly become aware of pangolins, along with their 'most trafficked' reputation. Many assume that the huge trade in pangolins is a new phenomenon. It is certain that the volume of animals now being harvested and traded is greater than ever, but records show that hunting and trading pangolins started way back.

Pangolins have long been exploited in Africa. In West Africa, all three locally occurring species are hunted, but the animal most often found in markets is the White-bellied pangolin. The Black-bellied and Giant pangolins are usually less commonly available, although there are regional variations. In East and southern Africa, pangolins have less local use than in Central and West Africa, and in southern Africa, only the Temminck's pangolin occurs.

Throughout Central and West Africa, pangolins are hunted both for bushmeat (i.e. consumption) and for medicinal and ritual purposes, with scales being prescribed for a wide variety of conditions ranging from leprosy to rheumatism. In Sierra Leone, 22 different pangolin body parts are used in the treatment of various conditions. In Benin the scales of White-bellied pangolins are used to prevent accidents and even to protect against gunshots. Throughout the region, pangolin products are used for warding off evil spirits, treating mental illness, bringing good luck and assisting with fertility.

In 2018 a scientific paper estimated that at least 400,000 pangolins were being harvested annually in Central Africa. In the DRC, Cameroon,

Gabon, Equatorial Guinea and the Republic of the Congo, pangolins – despite their protected status – are commonly found in markets and restaurants. Another study revealed that in Kisangani, in the DRC, the number of Giant pangolins in markets had increased sevenfold between the years 2002 and 2009.

Evidence indicates that harvesting pangolins for bushmeat and medicinal purposes at the current rate in Central and West Africa is likely to be unsustainable, even for local usage – let alone increased demands from international traffickers. Africa's human population is set to double in the next 30 years, creating a burgeoning local market for pangolin products. During the past couple of decades, as demand from the Far East has added to traditional local usage, prices for the four pangolin species in all their range states across Africa have increased sharply. Market forces point to the inevitable: that, without properly enforced protection laws, pangolins will increasingly be harvested, and will likely be pushed towards, or actually into, extinction in many areas.

Asiatic pangolins were being traded internationally, particularly in the Far East, long before the present century. Several tonnes of Sunda, or Malayan pangolin scales, were exported from Indonesia to China between 1925 and 1929, despite the species being protected. It is thought this could have involved up to 10,000 animals each year. In a report published in 1965 it was said that, between 1958 and 1964, over 60 tonnes of scales were exported from Indonesia to Singapore and Hong Kong, these shipments being mostly destined for China for use in Traditional Chinese Medicine. The figure of 60 tonnes probably represented over 160,000 pangolins.

In Taiwan between the 1950s and 1970s, pangolin leather was in great demand, and this trade is believed to have used 60,000 animals annually, which resulted in local pangolin population declines and prompting Taiwan to import the product from Southeast Asia. Each year throughout the 1970s, 50,000–60,000 Sunda or Malayan pangolins were imported to the island nation from Cambodia, Laos, Indonesia, Malaysia, Vietnam,

Examples of pangolin scale products seized by the Hong Kong government

Myanmar and the Philippines. The Taiwan trade closed in the 1980s due to a hunting ban, higher labour costs and increasing shortages of supply.

During the latter part of the last century, when the international trade in the Asiatic species of pangolin in Southeast Asia was already substantial, export trade in the four African species was still almost non-existent. Because there was little knowledge at this time regarding pangolin population sizes or birth rates, it was impossible to determine to what degree the trade in the Asian species was sustainable. However, a decline was observed in all four Asian species in all their range states. The incentive was there to exploit sources further afield.

The majority of trade in African species involves scales, which are hidden within cargo sent by both air and sea. Nigeria has been identified as the most frequently used export point, and Singapore and Malaysia are two of the main transit points for trade in pangolin scales en route to China and Vietnam. The surge in the illicit wildlife trade (not just pangolins) can, to some extent, be linked to the increase in general international trade and travel between Africa and Vietnam and the ever-growing number of Chinese immigrants into various African states. Poverty is often the driver at the hunter/poacher first level of the trade, and highly organised international criminal gangs at the other end ensure the efficient onward movement of wildlife products. This trafficking is a major factor in the decimation of many of Africa's wild species.

Illegal international trade in pangolins between July 2019 and August 2000 is estimated to involve nearly 900,000 individual animals. This estimate is based on the seizure of 1,474 shipments and records recovered from traffickers, so cannot be considered to represent the total number, which must be larger. It is thought likely that White-bellied pangolins made up the majority of the animals trafficked in this period. The bulk of illegal international trade in this 19-year period occurred in the later years, between 2016 and 2019, which indicates that the volume of trade is increasing.

When CITES was first constituted, in 1975, the pressures on pangolins were acknowledged and the Sunda (Malayan), Chinese and Indian species were all listed in Appendix II. Temminck's pangolin was included in Appendix I, and Ghana proposed listing the other three African species for Appendix III. Nevertheless, between 1975 and 2000, the trade in pangolins reported to CITES involved an estimated 776,000 animals – mostly Sunda pangolins, with less trade involving the Chinese and Indian species. The peaks in this trade were in 1981, at about 60,000, and 2000 with 74,000 skins. Although these figures may sound high, it is believed that the parallel unreported, and therefore illegal, trade was much greater.

The beginning of the new century heralded more protection for all pangolin species, but ever-increasing demand and lack of enforcement and implementation of CITES trade regulations has resulted in continuing declines. In 2000 at the CITES COP11, all four Asian pangolin species were included in Appendix I. Between 2000 and COP17 in 2016 (held in Johannesburg), trafficking in the four African species increased dramatically, and at COP17 these four species joined their Asian cousins already listed in Appendix I. Theoretically – and only theoretically – all internal trade in all eight pangolin species should now have stopped.

The reality is different, and is one of too many examples of the impotence of CITES if member states (Parties) ignore what they have signed up to. A range of punitive mechanisms can be used by the international community to punish states that act illegally or fail, in their own countries, to enforce laws they are party to. Once the Covid-19 pandemic has passed, it remains to be seen whether some sort of new world order will emerge. What can't be disputed is that, for many global issues, including the trade in wildlife, global solutions must be found, involving national governments ceding power to global governance mechanisms. International cooperation and enforcement of international laws regarding wildlife and the natural world would be a good place to start. Not only would this benefit pangolins and the rest of the natural world, it would help ensure human survival on the planet.

But judging by the political power posturing of the world's leading governments, this is still a long way off unless, together with a Covid-19 vaccine, medical science invents a 'grow up and get real' pill for the world's leaders!

Pangolins: Science, Society and Conservation, published by Academic Press, was the source for much of the data included in this chapter. In this book, and in Rachel Newer's book, *Poached*, the figure of $300 per kilogram for pangolin meat is mentioned. This was clearly the established market price at the time of writing, because it is precisely the same price that I was quoted by the restaurant I visited in Ho Chi Minh City in November 2019. This uniformity of prices does not only apply to pangolin meat, but also to tiger cake and other products. That prices are consistent and universal drives home the point that pangolins and other wildlife products are part of a market that is strongly regulated by crime syndicates operating with impunity across many Southeast Asian countries.

This Temminck's pangolin has found a cache of
insects under the bark of a tree. (Francois Meyer)

CHAPTER 14

THE FUTURE

Does the most trafficked mammal in the world have a future, or are the world's eight pangolin species heading for extinction, be it local or total? At the moment there is no really effective implementation and enforcement of the existing national and international laws designed to rescue pangolins from their perilous slide.

Many in the wildlife conservation sector believe that the implication of pangolins as possible vectors of Covid-19 between bats and humans will force China and other Southeast Asian countries to close their wet markets and prohibit consumption of wildlife species. For wild animals, the rest of the natural world – including humans – this would be the best possible outcome.

However, there is another sinister possibility: if creatures such as bats, civets, pangolins and many other such species come to be regarded as dangerous, disease-carrying threats, they could be targeted for elimination. This may sound far-fetched, but the record of human treatment of wildlife and the natural world is abysmal. After shark attacks it is common for there to be proposals to cull as many sharks as possible in order to reduce the occasional danger they pose to humans. When it became clear that the coronavirus outbreak was going to affect the world, and would not spare the United States of America, gun and ammunition sales in the USA rocketed to record levels. Did American gun and ammunition buyers think they could shoot the virus? Were they preparing in case they needed to shoot each other in the event of chaos and civil disorder? This reaction demonstrates that when humans get frightened, their reaction often is, 'Kill!'.

Instead of recognising that tampering with the natural world comes at a cost, humans continue to tamper and hope that medical science or guns and bullets will help us defeat nature when it fights back.

'If it pays it stays' is a widely touted strategy for ensuring a future for wildlife. For this to work, rural communities need to recognise that killing a wild animal is a one-time use, whereas ecotourism offers ongoing, sustainable reward. The value of *wild* wildlife, as opposed to *farmed* wildlife, will only be enthusiastically embraced when those people who have to live alongside it can also be sustained by it, and so choose to become its guardians and protectors. Farmed wildlife benefits only the farmers and their employees, whereas genuine wildlife can benefit not just those who live in its midst, but also whole ecosystems, and the economies of countries.

The desire to see pangolins is one of the main drawcards at places like the Tswalu Private Game Reserve. Alongside rigorous law enforcement, pangolin ecotourism offers a multi-use value to local people and tourists alike, and this mutually beneficial arrangement is key in the battle to defeat trafficking.

Pangolins are hunted for a range of uses: their leather is prized, their meat is highly rated, and their body parts and scales are processed for use in a wide variety of traditional medicines and customs. The complexity of the demand and the range of markets involved indicate that diverse law enforcement strategies will be needed. Community engagement, intelligence gathering, efficient liaison between the police forces of the countries involved, greater penalties for those convicted – all these and more are weapons in the law enforcement armoury, and all will have to work together to beat the scourge. In order to be effective, measures to control and ultimately stop the illicit trade will have to involve international organisations and individual nations working properly together. In the case of some consumer countries this will require a total re-set in their law-enforcement attitudes.

Criminal gangs don't respect borders, their main concern being how to smuggle illegal items across them. In contrast, international law enforcement agencies have to work with national police forces within existing frameworks and protocols, and often by the time strategies have been formulated, permissions granted and arrest warrants obtained, the criminals are long gone. That international law enforcement is a challenge is beyond doubt; what makes it that much more difficult and complex is the deliberate failure of some nations to make any real attempt to enforce the laws they have signed up to.

Interpol, CITES, the IUCN and all the other international bodies that are in any way involved in policing the illegal wildlife trade have an array of enforcement tools, and considerable powers at their disposal. However, lack of interest, corruption, low prioritisation, inadequate enforcement budgets and other factors all seriously impede efforts to catch the criminals, and in the complex world of international politics, governments are often not held to account.

Despite huge amounts of money spent over many decades and some serious commitment by governments to fight international narcotics dealing, drug producers and dealers continue to ply their trades and flourish. Pangolins and many other species and animal products are now, like drugs, worth so much money that people are prepared to risk their lives and imprisonment by taking part in the trade at various levels. However, the trade in illegal wildlife does not have remotely the same level of international commitment deployed against it as does the battle to combat drug trafficking, so the comparison produces a bleak picture.

Does the world's most trafficked mammal have a future or does extinction beckon? Revenge killing of this 'dangerous-to-human-health' animal is possible but unlikely. In the best-case scenario, the SARS Covid-19 outbreak will lessen the demand, and so also the supply of pangolins.

However, in April 2020, United Nations agencies predicted that, as a result of Covid-19, the number of starving people in the world could increase hugely and reach 250–300 million. Most people living in rich countries have never experienced starvation or seen it close up on a large scale. Had they done so, they would understand the desperation of the starving: when an animal, human or otherwise, is starving it will eat just about anything. If the number of those starving does sharply increase, the demand for bushmeat could likewise increase sharply. Pangolins will probably increasingly be hunted and consumed at local levels.

We might comfort ourselves that, as long as reserves such as Tswalu continue to exist, threatened species will be safe within them. They ensure, to some extent, the continued existence of the wildlife they harbour. We can hope that multi-use, living ecotourism wins out over the single-use capture-and-consume model, and that this will mitigate the effects of the likely increase in demand for bushmeat. Having said this, there's an alarming caveat: in order for this model to succeed, ecotourism needs to flourish. And the Covid-19 pandemic looks set to slow the growth of global travel and ecotourism for many years.

The pandemic is a global game changer. One of the outcomes is that humans are being given the chance to press some re-set buttons. During national lockdown periods, pollution levels reduced dramatically all over the world; wildlife trade (along with much other trade) diminished; people in rich countries started questioning their addiction to consumerism; enhanced local production reduced the movement of goods around the world; and many people in advanced countries started to re-evaluate how they spend their time and changed their lifestyles. These and many other issues point to the human race being given an opportunity, perhaps, to escape from what seemed a one-way, self-destructing system.

We could move forward, not into a perfect world, but into a world that has learnt a lesson – a world in which we live as part of, rather than apart from nature.

When I was interviewing the Bushman elder, Izak Kruiper, for his Foreword to this book, he said that whoever killed a pangolin would have bad luck. He would certainly find it credible that the coronavirus Covid-19 is the pangolin's way of striking back against human abuse of the species. When the Bushmen need rain, they invoke the spirit of the pangolin, singing pangolin rain songs to encourage the arrival of life-sustaining rain. It is a huge flight of fancy, but perhaps there's some validity to the view that Covid-19 is the fight-back strategy of the most trafficked wild mammal in the world – and that it might just have helped rescue it from extinction. In years to come when people look into the eye of the pangolin and become captivated by its magic – rather than capturing it for consumption – it could mean that, in learning to respect and protect wildlife, humans had, at last, found their full humanity, and ensured their own survival on the planet.

Kelsey Prediger- AfriCat Foundation

Dawn breaks over a new world?

EPILOGUE

In Zululand, in South Africa's KwaZulu-Natal province, Zambezi was out on his nightly foraging expedition. He was slowly making his way up a gentle rocky slope on the Phinda Private Game Reserve. Zambezi had settled in well and now it was as if he had never lived anywhere else. In Zimbabwe, his country of birth, he had lived in Matabeleland, populated by the Ndebele (Matabele) people. In the 1820s, under the leadership of Mzilikazi, a breakaway group left their Zulu homeland and moved north to what is now Matabeleland. Zambezi had exchanged homes the other way around when he was caught by Joseph, the Matabele poacher, and carried south, ending up in Zululand where his species had been locally extinct for around 90 years.

Now Zambezi picked his way carefully, totally engrossed in his search for ants, guided by his powerful sense of smell. Before his capture, the natural world had held few threats for him; and, although the memories of his capture and the suffering he had endured had faded, the ordeal meant that the presence of humans triggered an automatic increase in stress that would never completely disappear.

But all life is insecure and ephemeral, and having survived human predation was no guarantee that the pangolin was out of all danger. It was a clear night, and both the moon and starlight illuminated the little animal as he made his way up the slope between the rocks. Every now and then he made scratching noises as he dug for ants or investigated something that interested him.

A human observer might have been aware that they were watching the most trafficked mammal on earth. They might have known that the whole human world was in upheaval, thanks to a global pandemic, and that pangolins were suspected of being the carriers of the virus responsible for the chaos.

Zambezi was, of course, unaware of the notoriety now attached to the word 'pangolin'. His forebears have existed on earth for about

80 million years – quite a success story! In contrast, humans have been on the planet for just 200,000 years, only a fraction of the time; and to have put the future of our own species in danger in one four-hundredths of the time is a spectacular failure! Zambezi was not thinking of success or failure, he was thinking about ants.

"THEY DIDN'T LAST LONG, DID THEY ?!"

James (Wild Bill) Peirce

Other than from an ant or termite's perspective, pangolins are one of nature's most harmless, least aggressive creatures. The same cannot be said of humans. If he could think human thoughts, Zambezi would have been worried and disappointed; we can only hope he would have been forgiving. Unless humans very soon learn to live as part of nature, rather than trying to dismantle it, Mother Nature will not be as forgiving, and her eventual wrath will be terrible.

STOP PRESS

● In early June 2020 China's Health Times newspaper reported that the country's State Forestry and Grassland Administration (SFGA) had removed pangolin scales from an official 2020 listing of ingredients approved for use in Traditional Chinese Medicine. The delisting followed a move by the SFGA that raised the protected status of pangolins to the highest level with immediate effect.

Commentators and campaigners were hugely encouraged by the move, which they hoped would not only mean immediate increased protection for pangolins, but which also might indicate more general positive wildlife outcomes from the ongoing review process of China's Wildlife Protection Law. Steve Blake, chief representative of WildAid

Wildlife Conservation Society